John Kersley Fowler

Echoes of old County Life

Being Recollections of Sport, Politics, and farming in the good old Times

John Kersley Fowler

Echoes of old County Life

Being Recollections of Sport, Politics, and farming in the good old Times

ISBN/EAN: 9783337133733

Printed in Europe, USA, Canada, Australia, Japan

Cover: Foto ©ninafisch / pixelio.de

More available books at **www.hansebooks.com**

ECHOES

OF

OLD COUNTY LIFE,

BEING RECOLLECTIONS OF

*SPORT, POLITICS, AND FARMING IN THE
GOOD OLD TIMES.*

BY

J. K. FOWLER
Of Aylesbury.

LONDON: EDWARD ARNOLD,
37, BEDFORD STREET, STRAND, W.C.
Publisher to the India Office.
1892.

RICHARD CLAY & SONS, LIMITED,
LONDON & BUNGAY.

TO

THE RIGHT HON. SIR HARRY VERNEY,

WHO FOR MORE THAN SIXTY YEARS

HAS DONE MANY ACTS OF KINDNESS TO ME AND MY FAMILY,

I Dedicate this Book

AS A SLIGHT TRIBUTE OF RESPECT AND AFFECTION.

October, 1892.

CONTENTS.

CHAPTER I.

Introductory—Masters of the Buckhounds and other Eminent Sportsmen—Mowbray Morris and Lord Southampton—'Varsity Races, Roger Palmer and the Crimean Steeplechase—Professor Neate—The Romance of Cheslyn Hall—Lord Chesterfield and the Election of Speaker Abercrombie—Grant's Picture of the Royal Hunt—Count D'Orsay: his Change of Clothes, his Knife-spinning, and his Sketches ... ... *p.* 1

CHAPTER II.

Elections at the Time of the Reform Bill of 1832—Aylesbury Contests—"Potwallers" and the Ancient Franchise—Bribery and Treating—The Chiltern Hundreds—Anecdotes about Sir Richard Bethell: his Election Contests and Expulsion from the Conservative Club—A "Tie" between Smith and Wentworth—My Hunt Breakfast—How Arkwright made his Fortune—Lord Nugent's Election Fights—Winthrop Praed—Voters and Refreshments: Curious Account-keeping—Amersham Elections and the Reward for the Fair ... *p.* 20

CHAPTER III.

Disraeli's Early Political History—His Election Contest at High Wycombe, and an old Radical Diary—The Story of his Early Radicalism—His Chartist Speech and Repartees on the Hustings—His Noisy Reception at Aylesbury—His Agricultural Foibles—Fawcett, the Comedian—Disraeli on Bob Lowe—His Famous Breakdown—His Boyish Prophecy ... *p.* 42

CHAPTER IV.

Bulgarian Atrocities in Buckinghamshire—Lord Beaconsfield's Speech in the Corn Exchange at Aylesbury and Rothschild's Opinion of it—Disraeli and the Cattle Defence Association—Disraeli and Protection—At Hughenden: its Cedars, its Purchase—Mrs. Disraeli's Frugality—The Romantic Story of Miss Williams' Legacy—Disraeli as Chancellor of the Exchequer—His Manchester Speech—His Opinion of the Disfranchising Act of 1832—His Sympathy for the Agricultural Labouring Class, their Earnings, their Right of Combination—On Publicans and "Exhausted Volcanoes"—His Death and Funeral *p.* 59

CHAPTER V.

Bordeaux and Epernay in 1868—An Incident at Chambord—Messrs. Nathaniel Johnstone: their Vineyards at Dausac—The Manufacture of Claret—Mr. Moët's Vineyards at Epernay—The Manufacture of Champagne—National Tastes in Wine—Longevity—"Ways and Means" Lowndes ... ... *p.* 79

CHAPTER VI.

Steeplechasing in the Year 1835—The Great Race at Aylesbury: Captain Beecher wins from Mr. Allnutt—The Races the Year following: Jem Mason is too clever—The Royal Hunt Club; Anecdotes of a Horse in their Dining-Room—Anecdotes of the Rev. C. Erle and Bishop Wilberforce—Mr. Carroll's Horses, Family, and Jokes ... ... *p.* 89

CHAPTER VII.

Louis XVIII. at Hartwell—The English Garden—The King has his own again; my Father escorts him to London—The Manners of Parochial Clergy—Tate and Brady triumphant—Horsewhipping a Miller—An Independent Tory—Anecdote of Lord Palmerston and the Witty Bishop ... ... *p.* 104

CHAPTER VIII.

Prison Discipline Fifty Years Ago—Sweeping the Streets of Aylesbury—Old Jem and his Bill—Description of the County

Prison—Murderers and their Beer—Attempted Escapes—John Tawell, Quaker; his Trial for Murder and his previous Career—"Apple-pip" Kelly—Imprisonment for Debt—Captain Paulet and "Tally ho! Hanmer" ... ... *p.* 115

CHAPTER IX.

The "Rochester Room" at the White Hart, Aylesbury—Its Decoration and History—The Glories of Eythrope—Sir Walter Scott—Vernon's Anecdotes about Turner—Anecdotes of Landseer—"Swill" from Her Majesty's Kitchens—Charles Gow—A Pun and its Interpretation by *Punch* ... ... *p.* 134

CHAPTER X.

The Railway Mania—George Hudson, the Railway King—Serving Notices in Ireland—Railway Enterprise and Landlords—George Stephenson and the "Eldest Child"—In Coaching Days—Old Times in Winter—Dr. Lee's Prophecies and their Fulfilment—The late Duke of Buckingham and Chandos: an Uphill Fight—Stowe in Days of Prosperity—The Queen's Visit—In Days of Adversity—Sir Thomas Aubrey as an Upright Judge—Sir John Aubrey and his Dinners for the Free and Independent
p. 148

CHAPTER XI.

University Steeplechase Meeting at Banbury—A Nasty Brook—A Famous Race over the Broughton Farm—A Horse comes Upstairs—Leech Manning rides the little Grey Mare over the Dining-room Table—Gambling and Betting—A Captain who pursued Welshers—Of a Fool and his Folly—A Salt-water Tragedy ... ... *p.* 168

CHAPTER XII.

Fox-Hunting and Stag-Hunting—A fine Run with "the Baron"—Lord Lonsdale's Harriers and the Cumberland Bagmen—The Ballad of "The Captive Fox"—Jack Hannan *v.* Johnny Broome—Men of Peace and War—An Innocent Child, and a Clever Clearance ... ... *p.* 183

CONTENTS.

CHAPTER XIII.

The Vienna Exhibition of 1873   A Sturdy English Watch—The Emperor admires my Bull—A Contrast in Costume—The Paris Exhibition of 1878—Four-horned Sheep—Rosa Bonheur visits the Cattle—Foot-and-Mouth Disease—The Projected Palestine Canal—*The Times* condemns it—Its Route, its Cost, its Future   ...   .   *p.* 197

CHAPTER XIV.

Posting on the Great North Road—Bob Newman of Regent Street—Old "Boys"—Loyal Tom King of Amersham; he drives King George III.—An Elopement and the Sequel—May-Day Procession of the Mails—The Railway Fiend—The Wisdom of Weller—Old London Inns—An English Bill of Fare and the *Menu à la Russe*—The Old Norfolk Circuit—The Bar Mess: Fitzroy Kelly *v.* Serjeant Storks—One Pint many Times—Puritan Ipswich—A Peccant Engine ...   .   *p.* 210

CHAPTER XV.

Shorthorn Breeding—The Byles Dinners—Lord Dunmore to the Rescue—Eminent Breeders in the Palmy Days—My Sale and Sales in General—The Rose of the Quarter Sessions—A Dissertation on Poultry—The Prebendal Geese—The Aylesbury Duckling—A Year of Wet and a Year of War—A Legal Decision on Crops   ...   .   *p.* 230

CHAPTER XVI.

A Poor Law Guardian—The Curse of Out-door Relief—The Fortunes of Agriculture—Harvest Homes—Allotments and Gardens—Steam and Spade—The Virtues of Co-operation Since 1830—The Swing Riots—Cottage Accommodation—The Smock Frock and the Black Coat—The Archdeacon and Potatoes—The Better Part   ...   .   *p.* 244

ILLUSTRATIONS.

PORTRAIT OF MR. J. K. FOWLER   *Frontispiece*

THE JUMP OVER THE DINNER-TABLE   *To face page* 174

"KING CHARMING," SHORTHORN BULL. From a drawing by HARRISON WEIR   *To face page* 234

ECHOES

OF

OLD COUNTY LIFE.

CHAPTER I.

Introductory—Masters of the Buckhounds and other Eminent Sportsmen—Mowbray Morris, and Lord Southampton—'Varsity Races, Roger Palmer and the Crimean Steeplechase—Professor Neate—The Romance of Cheslyn Hall—Lord Chesterfield and the Election of Speaker Abercrombie—Grant's Picture of the Royal Hunt—Count D'Orsay: his Change of Clothes, his Knife-spinning, and his Sketches.

THESE "Reminiscences" differ from others that have hitherto been published, in being those, not of men like Lord Malmesbury, Captain Gronow, the Hon. Grantley Berkeley, Mr. Greville, and others who belonged to the upper classes of society; nor of legal luminaries, such as Serjeant Ballantine or Mr. Montagu Williams; nor of a man renowned upon the stage or with the brush, but of a fair representative of middle-class life who, in the course of a busy career, has met many famous people, and here truthfully records what he remembers about them. I believe these records give a faithful picture of the times in which I have lived; and, while I hope they will be interesting and amusing, I may without vanity say that they have also an historical value, depicting as they do a series of events—social, sporting, literary, agricultural, and political—which stirred many thousands of minds in the middle of the nineteenth century.

Amongst many of my recollections are some which may interest my readers, as bringing before them the names of several who have arrived at great eminence in the State, or in the general whirl of society. I remember when the late Lord Granville was Master of the Buckhounds, and I dare say many there are who would hardly believe that that eminent and courteous statesman began his public career in the above sporting capacity. I rode with him on one occasion to a meet at Creslow to show him the way there, as he had arrived from London after the hounds had left Aylesbury, and shall not forget the delightful six-mile ride I had with him: his conversation, his courteous manners, the pleasure he felt at the beauty of our Vale, and especially at the view from the hills where the deer was uncarted. Shortly after the start Lord Canning, afterwards Viceroy of India, who always went in the first flight, charged a strong post-and-rail fence, and his horse, striking the top beam, came down, throwing his rider heavily. He lay motionless, and I jumped off my horse and called for assistance. We raised him up, loosened his collar, bathed his head and face with water, and he slowly regained consciousness. We took him to an adjoining farm-house, and after about an hour he was sufficiently recovered to return to Aylesbury, and was in the saddle again the next day as well as ever.

. I remember also Lord Kinnaird as Master of the Buckhounds. He afterwards became the leader of a religious party in London for some years, and his name is still remembered by many Exeter Hall *habitués*, who little thought he had ever held such a post of worldly pastime. It was generally considered that this nobleman was the chief cause of the gradual break-up of the visit of the Royal pack to Aylesbury. He used to bring with him his wife, and they lived quietly in their private rooms at the White Hart. The jovial meetings of the Royal Hunt Club, thus deserted by the gallant Master, lost their charm, and the dinner-party rapidly diminished, as there was no centre round which they could rally after the day's sport was ended, and no company to recount the deeds of flood and field that might have distinguished it. The late Lord Rosslyn, as Master, I shall not forget, nor how, in riding home after a most severe run with a heavy and blinding storm of hail and sleet driving into our faces, my horse trod on the toe of a hound, causing him to cry out and whimper, when his lordship, who was a very quick-tempered man, blew me up in no very measured terms, till my good friend, Charles Davis, the Royal huntsman, came to my aid; and in the evening Lord Rosslyn apologized to me for his hasty temper.

Another and most popular Master I knew and have enjoyed a ride with—I mean Lord Cork; and I shall not forget him, as Lord Dungarvan, riding over our farm in the Broughton country at one of the Oxford "'Varsity" steeplechases, and seeing him go for the last two miles in the most dashing style without his cap, as he had lost it in charging a tremendous bullfincher, where it hung upon a prickly whitethorn about ten feet high. I think he ran third, out of a field of fourteen. The race was won by Mr. H. Blundell, who afterwards distinguished himself in the Crimea, and is now a colonel and was a member of the late House of Commons. Another time that I met Lord Cork in the saddle was in Lord Carrington's park at High Wycombe, the last day poor Charles Davis hunted Her Majesty's hounds, as he had a severe fall over the wire of a telegraph pole, and, I think, never recovered sufficiently to hunt the pack again.

Many amusing episodes rise to my mind as I recall memories of men long passed away, and of others still living. One of the most accomplished and most agreeable men it was ever my lot to meet was the late Mr. Mowbray Morris, the then financial manager of the *Times*. He was a remarkably handsome man, faultlessly dressed and perfect in his "get up," rode good horses—which he kept at Winslow with Harry Poole, the great arbiter of fashion in Savile Row,—and hunted generally with Lord Southampton's hounds and "Squire Drake's," but often with "the Baron." He was not a good horseman, and one day his horse, soon after the start, got the better of him, and carried him unwittingly amongst the pack. Lord Southampton, who often used very strong language, and would never submit to any breach of hunting manners, rode after him, and yelled out, "Hold hard, you —— printer!" His lordship had decided in his mind that any one connected with *The Times* must necessarily be a printer.

When the 'Varsity Races were over the Broughton

country, there was a race in which young Roger Palmer, now Sir Roger, distinguished himself less than he afterwards did before Sebastopol. He rode a mare of old George Symonds', called The Parson's Daughter, a screw, but a famous fencer. Roger Palmer was a good-looking youngster, but noted for having a very big head, quite out of proportion to his body. The mare got well off, maintained her lead to near the end, and was so far ahead in the last field but one that her rider eased her, jumped into the winning field, and pulled her up into a walk, intending to pass quietly between the winning flags. The Hon. Mr. Portman was riding Joe Tollitt's horse, Valiant, and seeing his opportunity, he made a tremendous rush. Amidst the shouts of the spectators poor Palmer tried to put his mare into a gallop; but alas! it was too late, and Valiant won by a short neck, amidst roars of laughter. Some one came up to Palmer and said, "I always knew you would be beaten; you never had *head* enough to win a race."

I am reminded by the mention of Sir Roger Palmer's name, of the delight with which we saw in the papers of the day that the great Crimean Steeplechase was won by Blundell, Dewar coming in second, both old 'Varsity riders and winners of races, keeping up the prestige of our Broughton and Aylesbury courses. And, indeed, those courses were no easy ones to negotiate: once, when showing the riders over the course at Broughton, Lord Ribblesdale and some others loudly proclaimed the improbability of any horse jumping the brook. They were all walking, but I was on my favourite mare, who was well known by my friends (but not by the 'Varsity riders) as a marvellous water-jumper. One and all they objected to this water-jump, till I remarked, "Well, I am only on an ordinary hunter, and she shall jump it in her snaffle-bridle, without whip or spur." They declared it an impossibility. I was too careful of my own neck to risk it myself, but called to one of my neighbours, a plucky farmer, one of the best light-weights I ever saw cross a country, who knew my mare's prowess well, and I asked him to ride her. He willingly did so, mounted her, took her back about three hundred yards, shook her up, and she flew the hurdles which were in front of the brook, and landed safely over it on her hind legs, never wetting her heels, and went on in her gallop without noticing it. After this there could be no objection, and the race took place. The result was that out of fifteen starters eleven of them got into the water, and the others stoutly refused, two of them precipitating their riders over their heads into the middle of it; but as it was easy getting out, the race continued, and a fine finish was the result, Mr. Goldingham, I think, being declared winner. The jump of my mare was measured, and it was found she had cleared twenty-nine and a half feet.

A most amusing feature of one University Meeting was the prowess of Professor Neate, Professor of Political Economy at Oxford, and at one time Member of Parliament for that city. The dons and heads of houses were determined to put down steeplechasing, but old Neate stood up for the undergraduates; and, to show his contempt for their rulers, entered his own horse for one of the principal races, and named him "Vice-Chancellor." The day of the race came, and great doubts were raised as to who would be the jockey to steer the noted quadruped, when, to the astonishment of every one, the Professor himself appeared in a top-hat, and in his shirt-sleeves and black trousers. Amidst shouts of laughter the start was effected, and "the observed of all observers" took several fences well till the famous water-jump came in view, which his horse first refused, and then fell with his rider plump into the middle of, sousing him over head and ears. The Professor went no farther, but consoled himself by saying he had made his protest against the Heads of Houses, and vindicated the rights of the students to enjoy a manly sport.

In the early days of stag-hunting in the Vale with Baron Rothschild's hounds, two gentlemen were conspicuous by the splendour of their stud and the style and completeness of their establishments. To mention the names of Cheslyn Hall and Sam Baker to many persons now living is to recall to their memories the geniality of their manners, their open-handed liberality, the jollity and good-humour of their conversation, and the "all-round" popularity of their sporting careers. Cheslyn Hall—or, as he was generally called, "Chess"—was the younger brother of a firm of solicitors in New Court, Lincoln's Inn. Their father had established a high-class business, supported by several aristocratic and rich clients, and was succeeded by the two brothers, Henry and Cheslyn. Samuel Baker was a son of the head of the well-known firm of Baker and Sons, contractors and builders—their contract for the Government for the construction of the Keyham Docks at Devonport alone came to some millions sterling. Sam had an elder brother George, who had a fine hunting establishment with Mr. Henry Hall in Northamptonshire, with about twelve first-class hunters, and a household second to none in the neighbourhood. The other two brothers had their establishment at Tring for the Vale of Aylesbury. About the year 1851 Samuel Baker and Cheslyn Hall shifted their quarters to Aylesbury, building excellent loose-boxes for twenty hunters, fitted up with every convenience, with groom's house, harness- and saddle-rooms, boiling-houses, and everything the most fastidious Master of Horse could require. They took up their abode at the White Hart—then the most noted house in the Midlands—and ordered rooms, in addition to their own, for the Hon. Robert Grimston, Johnny Bell, and the well-known steeplechase rider, Jem Mason. They and their guests lived luxuriously on rare viands and the most noted vintage wines: if there was one thing more than another they prided themselves on, it was the glorious port of the vintages 1820, '26, and '34. These gentlemen—Messrs. Hall and Baker—were at the head of every subscription for promoting sport, agricultural shows, charitable or other useful works in the neighbourhood; yet such was their recklessness and extravagance that old-fashioned people looked askance and said an end would soon come to this extraordinary expenditure. At the end of the hunting season about twenty of their horses were sent to Tattersall's, where they realized what were then immense prices, several making 300, 350, and 400 guineas each.

After these gentry had kept the game alive at Aylesbury for some years, it was announced that Mr. Baker was going to be married to a Miss Burnand, the beautiful daughter of a well-known Stock Exchange financier, and about the end of the season a large party of ladies and gentlemen were invited down to view the combined stud and establishment, to take a last farewell of the bachelorhood of the well-known Samuel Baker, and to duly celebrate the break-up of the sporting home of those two distinguished sportsmen. A superb luncheon was provided in the "Rochester" room at the White Hart, and the lawns and pleasure-grounds were filled by a large company of exquisitely-dressed and beautiful women, amongst whom the future bride was not the least fair. It was in the month of April, and peaches and nectarines at £3 3s. a dozen, strawberries at 16s. a pound, ices, and every costly luxury graced the board. After waiting some time it was noticed that no Cheslyn Hall appeared on the scene, to the surprise of all present, and of Mr. Baker especially. The company, after visiting the stud, returned to London; the stud was removed to Tattersall's, and, as usual, made great prices; the saddles, bridles, horse-cloths, and all the appurtenances of the establishment disappeared from the scene. After some weeks rumours got afloat that debts owing in the town had not been paid: this was unusual, as everything hitherto had been most punctually settled month by month. One morning an announcement appeared in *The Times*, with a flaming leading article, that the great firm of solicitors, the Brothers Hall, had become bankrupt, with a deficiency of over £67,000; that moneys received by them for clients had been appropriated to their own uses; that the extravagance of their establishment at Neasden, where they kept a stud for breeding hunters and cart-horses and a pack of harriers, the hunting establishment of Cheslyn at Aylesbury, and of Henry at Kilsby, in Northamptonshire, to say nothing of two separate homes for the brothers and their ladies in London, mainly accounted for the serious deficiencies in their accounts. Sir Charles Rushout was the principal sufferer; he had such implicit confidence in the Halls that he actually committed his banking account into their hands, with power to draw on it as they wished. One specially hard case came to light, which was the ultimate cause of the utter collapse of the firm. A widow lady, who was one of their clients, was persuaded by them to sell her all, about £1200 from the Three per Cents., that they might put it out on mortgage at 5 per cent. Cheslyn went with her to the Bank of England, and the whole was sold out and handed over to him in bank-notes. He placed the lady in a cab and drove with her towards his offices to complete the mortgage; but in Fleet Street he suddenly stopped the cab and told her he saw a gentleman he was particularly anxious to talk to, and would be with her in New Court in a quarter of an hour. The unsuspecting widow sat in the cab about half an hour, and then getting tired, dismissed the driver, and went into the office and waited for over an hour more, still not imagining for a moment anything was wrong. She left word she could remain no longer, and went home to her hotel; next morning she again appeared at the office, but, finding neither of the Messrs. Hall had arrived, for the first time she became frightened and communicated with her friends. The Halls never came back to their office, and their whole business came to an end. I believe the poor widow received about 5*s.* in the £; Mr. Cheslyn Hall had appropriated £1000 of her fortune to stave off some pressing claims, and had kept the remainder for his own uses.

If it had not been for this disgraceful transaction some sort of sympathy would have been felt for the Halls, as it was discovered that at the death of their father the estate was already hopelessly insolvent. After the utter wreck of the firm the brothers went abroad, and were maintained by the subscriptions of their old friends and by the former recipients of their bounty and hospitality. The Hon. R. Grimston sent Cheslyn many a five-pound note, and Mr. Sam Baker, who himself had been shamefully treated by his friend, supported him for some time. At last it was found that this reckless lawyer was living on his wits somewhere on the sea-coast of Devonshire; that his easy, agreeable manners, his good looks, and the peculiar faculty he had of ingratiating himself with all with whom he came in contact, gave him the *entrée* into such society as he could find there. Amongst others, the captain of the Coastguard service became his patron, introduced him to his friends, and a right good time Cheslyn Hall had, till at last one and the other began to compare notes, when it was found that he had borrowed money of his new friends all round—from some £5, some £10, and from others one or two sovereigns at a time—and the captain was desired to inform him that they must part friends, and that he had better remove to another sphere. Cheslyn Hall had been lodging in a snug little cottage, and had given out that he was daily expecting heavy remittances from London. When he found he could no longer remain in the district he went home: when the next morning his landlady went into his room, as he had not come down at his usual time, she found him dead on his bed, with an empty phial marked "poison" in his hand. Thus ended the gay, joyous life of one who had been the pampered and petted child of fortune, and who had done as much to establish the Rothschild hounds in the Vale of Aylesbury as even the noted Barons themselves.

At the close of the year 1835 Sir Robert Peel dissolved Parliament, and the great trial of strength of the parties was to be on the Speakership. The King's staghounds were at Aylesbury the first week in February of the next year; Lord Chesterfield was Master of the Buckhounds. I remember well that Lord Chesterfield was in the chair at this dinner of the Royal Hunt Club, in the great room at the White Hart at Aylesbury. There was a brilliant assemblage; amongst the party were the Count D'Orsay, Lords F. and A. Fitzclarence, the Marquis of Clanricarde, Sir Horace Seymour, Sir Seymour Blanc, Hon. A. Arundel, Mr. (afterwards Sir Geo.) Wombwell, Johnny Bushe, Col. Standen, Captain Fairlie, Mr. De Burgh, the master of the rival pack of staghounds which hunted the Vale on alternate days with the Royal pack, the Vyses, the Harcourts, the Learmonths, the Seymours, the Sieverights, Harry Peyton, Shakerley, Newdegate, and many of the gayest men about town, over forty in all, ardent sportsmen. Betting had been the order of the day for many weeks as to the issue of the Parliamentary contest, the old Speaker, Manners-Sutton, representing the Ministry, and Mr. Abercrombie the Whigs. No railway or telegraph was then in existence, and the express as to the issue of the struggle was sent down by post-boy, stage by stage, and the argument was at its height when the clatter of the post-horse was heard in the yard. Well do I remember mine host (I can see him now) taking the sealed despatch up to the Earl in the chair, while wild excitement prevailed, and wagers were shouted across the table. The Earl broke the seals and his countenance fell; I heard him say, " Gentlemen, it's all over. Abercrombie, 312; Sutton, 302 " (I think these were the numbers). " I shall no longer be Master of the Buckhounds." I never saw such an alteration from the extreme of gaiety to that of despondency. The Earl was the most popular sportsman at that time in England, and I think in about six weeks the Ministry resigned.

These were indeed brilliant times for Aylesbury: never was such a gathering of noble sportsmen assembled together as used to meet at the White Hart, when the King's and Mr. De Burgh's staghounds came down for the week in November and in February and hunted alternate days. Nothing had ever been seen before or since like it. The hotel was not only filled, but the proprietor took as many private houses in the town as he could procure. I remember one of these contained Lords Erroll, A. and F. Fitzclarence, and their friend, Poodle Wombwell; another, Count D'Orsay, H. Baring, Whyte Melville, and Sir Horace Seymour; a third, the Marquis of Waterford, Lord William Beresford, and two others ; a fourth, Lords Gardner and Powerscourt ; and others billeted wherever a good bed was to be found. At the hotel stayed Earl Chesterfield, the Prince Trautzmandorff, Hon. A. Arundel, Mr. De Burgh, Mr. Shakerley, Lords C. Paget, Cranstoun, Ossulton, Cantelupe, and Jocelyn. Stabling and forage were provided for more than 160 hunters, and the George, which entertained the "Second String," was also full. The following is a list of the Royal Hunt Club which was formed at the White Hart, Aylesbury, in the year 1835—President, the Master of the Buckhounds for the time being ; First President, Earl of Chesterfield ; Lords Frederick and Augustus Fitzclarence, Marquis of Clanricarde, Earl of Erroll, Count D'Orsay, Colonel Sir Horace Seymour, Colonel Sir Seymour Blane, Hon. A. Arundel, Lieut.-Colonel Standen, Captains Halford and Cosbey, Messrs. De Burgh, Wombwell, Bushe, Hawkins, Harcourt, G. Vyse, W. Vyse, Henry Bainbridge, Walter Learmonth, Thomas Learmonth, Henry Seymour, Shakerley, Newdegate, Carroll, Captains Sieveright and Fairlie. Many names were afterwards added to these, while on the Presidential roll as Masters of the Buckhounds I remember the Earl of Erroll till 1839 ; Lord Kinnaird, 1840 ; Lord Rosslyn, 1841 ; Earl Granville, 1846.

It was a fine sight to see the horses led round the market square in the morning, after breakfast, and brought up one by one to the portico of the hotel and there mounted by their owners. The street was soon filled with scarlet coats, and carriages and four, and all sorts and conditions of conveyances going to the meet.

On one occasion when the meet was at Burston, it was computed that more than 2000 horsemen were present, and when the mass of horsemen charged the first fence, a new stake and binder, the whole fence fell flat, scores of riders having landed or fallen upon it.

I was present when it was proposed to have the celebrated picture of the Royal Hunt painted. The idea was mooted at the dinner-table, when Mr. Grant, the artist, was present, who was a good man across the Vale, and an excellent sportsman. Lord Chesterfield was in the chair, and it was agreed by all present that they would sit for their portraits, and that the picture should represent the meet at Creslow, one of the most popular in the Vale, where at that time the Duke of Grafton's foxhounds also met, and where now that veteran sportsman, Selby Lowndes, shows plenty of sport. The house is a very fine, interesting mediæval structure, formerly a portion of the ancient monastery of Christ Low. It belongs now, as it did then, to Lord de Clifford, in whose family it has been for centuries, and it is the reputed birthplace of poor ill-fated Rosamond Clifford, the "Fair Rosamond" of Henry II. A sketch of the place was taken, and the groups were designed, but before the picture was finished it was thought more appropriate to have the scene laid at Ascot Heath within sight of the kennels. Sir Francis Grant (late President of the Royal Academy) is to be seen in the picture behind Sir George Seymour, who is talking to Mr. Shifnel. The noble master, the handsome Earl of Chesterfield, is in the centre on his horse Sir Oliver, with his official couples on his shoulder. In front of him stands Lord Erroll, a nobleman all over; near him the handsome Count D'Orsay, whip in hand, his scarlet coat thrown open, showing his white waistcoat, his richly-embroidered satin scarf, his irreproachable leathers and boots; he is talking to the Duke of Beaufort, who is turning round on his horse to listen. Lord Adolphus is in this group, and Mr. Wombwell speaking to him. Messrs. Shakerley, H. Baring, and others are near at hand; Sir Horace Seymour seated on the ground; the veteran Charles Davis, the King's huntsman, on his noted gray, The Hermit, while grouped at his feet are the hounds, Old Governor, a rare favourite, with his tail curled over his back, Minstrel, a grand hound, of rather large size, in the extreme foreground, and close to him the fleet Dairymaid. Riding, to the centre of the picture, are Sir Andrew Barnard and the Earl of Wilton, who with loosened rein is tapping Sir Andrew on the arm, and apparently beating time as though humming a tune. Lord Frederick Fitzclarence faces the spectator; Mr. Learmonth, with the one-armed sporting farmer, William Nash, in attendance. Behind these is the artist, then Mr. Grant; and to the left are Sir Seymour Blane and Mr. W. Carroll, talking to "Paddy," on foot,—an Irishman who always ran with the hounds, and was generally well up at the finish. Many other portraits are there, and the picture is as much an historical one as if it portrayed a meeting of a Cabinet or a debate in the Houses of Parliament.

The Count D'Orsay was the life of the party at Aylesbury, full of animal spirits, certainly one of the finest and handsomest men I ever saw; he seemed, as did his companions, to abandon fashionable restraint, and give themselves up to rollicking schoolboy enjoyment when they came to the White Hart. "Knife-spinning" after dinner was one great source of fun. The Count and Mr. Peyton, afterwards Sir Henry, were the two generally pitted against each other, one on each side of the table ; the knives, selected by themselves, were well balanced, and at a given signal were set going by a swift twirl, and the betting commenced. I have seen scores of pounds lost over each match. When the Count had won, which was often the case, he was very liberal to the servants in attendance ; and I remember once on his leaving late at night, his carriage and four post-horses standing at the front door to take him to London, he distributed his sovereigns so plentifully that, happening to be in the hall, I too, as a boy, scrambled for and secured one of them, much to my delight. On one occasion, when he had only come prepared to stay two days, he was persuaded to prolong his visit, and he sent for the host and said, "What am I to do? I have no more clothes here except what I wore yesterday and to-day." My father said that of course they would do again. "No, no," replied the Count ; "I must not appear at the meet in the same dress again. You must send an express to London for my valet to bring a change of dress ;" and off went Humphrey, the old post-boy, on a saddle-horse to Mayfair, with a letter to his valet to come prepared for the next day. This was about six o'clock in the evening, and I recollect old Humphrey telling me that he had three horses on the road, changing at Berkhampstead and Watford, and

C

arrived in town, forty miles, by ten o'clock; found the valet had gone to Drury Lane Theatre; went there and brought him off; and by nine o'clock the next morning, in a yellow post-chaise and pair, came the valet with a change of costume for Sir Count, who appeared in full hunting panoply, radiant with smiles, the admired of all admirers, at the meet at Aston Abbotts. This freak of fashion must have cost him at least £10, as the railway was not then opened, and posting was a heavy item. The old cook, who had come from Merton College, Oxford, when my father, Mr. Fowler, first came to Aylesbury, more than twenty years previous, was pronounced by the Count, who called his friends around him and walked into the kitchen to show them, "the finest specimen of the English cook he had ever seen in his life." Poor old cook! He was indeed a wonder, living forty-seven years at the White Hart, where, single-handed, he has sent up dinners for 400 guests, and never a sauce or condiment forgotten. He was known to every nobleman and gentleman in the county, and was one of the best servants a master ever had.

The Earl of Erroll was a most popular Master of the Buckhounds, and his brothers-in-law, Lords Frederick and Adolphus, were always with him at the Aylesbury meetings; the latter a most wonderful likeness to his father, King William IV. Neither of them were good men over so stiff a country as the Vale of Aylesbury, but their genial manner, their handsome, good-natured countenances, and the splendid style of all their appointments, made them well noted in the field and in the town. It was a fine sight to see the assemblage seat themselves at dinner in the old Rochester Room at the White Hart, more than half of them in scarlet dress coats, the Count D'Orsay in a scarlet coat with a rather large roll collar thrown very much back, showing a broad expanse of white waistcoat, the coat lined and faced with pale blue satin, and the skirts with rich white watered silk. Dress was an art as well as expense in the old times. Oftentimes after dinner the conversation waxed fast and furious; the party would break up into twos and threes and recount the doings of the day. Then the Count would take some sheets of paper, and with a pen and ink sketch the portraits of many of the club with the most perfect touch and accuracy, and pass the sketches silently round the table, from one to the other, till they arrived at the persons represented, who would start with astonishment on recognizing their own portraits. So little was thought of these scraps of paper, that when the party broke up the waiters, on clearing the tables, would throw these fugitive pieces behind the fire with the *débris* from the dessert plates, and burn what would now be gems of value.

CHAPTER II.

Elections at the Time of the Reform Bill of 1832—Aylesbury Contests—"Potwallers" and the Ancient Franchise—Bribery and Treating—The Chiltern Hundreds—Anecdotes about Sir Richard Bethell: his Election Contests and Expulsion from the Conservative Club—A "Tie" between Smith and Wentworth—My Hunt Breakfast—How Arkwright made his Fortune—Lord Nugent's Election Fights—Winthrop Praed—Voters and Refreshments: Curious Account-keeping—Amersham Elections and the Reward for the Fair.

FROM my earliest boyhood I have taken great interest in the politics of the day. During the trying period of 1831-32, when the Reform mania was raging, we boys at school took sides, following for the most part the opinion of our fathers. I found myself as a Tory in a miserable minority, for the wave of revolution and reform passed over England just as it did in France, although without the violence and bloodshed which characterizes political crises with our brethren across the Channel. Still, the upheaving of the masses showed itself in the agrarian outrages and the "Swing" riots, and when the first Reform Bill was thrown out in the House of Lords, a torrent of violent abuse burst forth, and at the General Election which ensued party spirit ran high; the cry of "The Bill, the whole Bill, and nothing but the Bill," was the rallying-cry of the Reform party, of the Whigs led by Lords Grey, Brougham, and John Russell, of the Radicals who followed Jos. Hume, Tom Duncombe, and Cobbett, assisted by the Irish, under their chief, Dan O'Connell.

The "great historic County of Bucks," so named, and rightly, by its future greatest ornament, Benjamin Disraeli, was not behindhand in getting excited; every borough except Amersham was contested, even the little borough of Wendover, always considered a snug pocket-borough of the Smiths (the Carrington family), was fought by two candidates, Messrs. Burge and Camac, Liverpool merchants, in opposition to Abel Smith and his brother. The poll lasted two days, and the two latter were of course returned, the numbers being—A. Smith, 78; S. Smith, 77; Burge, 37; Camac, 36.

Aylesbury was the scene of a lively contest. The two old members, both Reformers (Lord Nugent and Mr. Rickford, the banker), were opposed by Viscount Kirkwall, the son of the Earl of Orkney, who resided at Taplow. The contest was really between the two lords, Mr. Rickford receiving the second votes of the electors of both parties. Lord Nugent was of a big, burly build, and Lord Kirkwall a very little man; and the contest was called the battle between "Little David" and the "Giant Goliath." The poll was kept open for five days, and resulted in the return of the old members. The contest was fought under the old franchise, and as the Three Hundreds of Aylesbury had been about thirty years before attached to the Borough, it was like a County election. Some of the voters had to be brought up for more than fifteen miles to record their votes. The polling for the County and Borough went on simultaneously, the town being crowded from morning till night with many hundreds of voters, with their friends, all of these folk eating and drinking either at the candidates' or some one else's expense, the cost to each candidate being enormous.

It will be noticed that I alluded just now to the old franchise. The Borough, as well as the Hundreds, voted under the most ancient of all the franchises, viz., as "Potwallers" or "Potwallopers." A "Potwaller" was a man who boiled his own pot on his own hearth, but who was not in receipt of parish relief. This was even more than household suffrage, and nearly approached universal suffrage, as two families might occupy one house; but if it were divided in occupation, and each head of the family boiled his own pot, he was a voter. This franchise was considered as old as Alfred the Great, and was looked upon as a great privilege; and my father, who was a freeholder, a renter, and a householder, always registered for many years after, up to the time of his death, on the old franchise. At the passing of the Reform Bill this franchise, with others—such as those enjoyed by freemen and freeholders, whether resident or not—was retained, and I think there are still two or three people living who are registered under it. The late Lord Beaconsfield always considered the great Reform Bill of 1832 as a disfranchising Bill, and, although he kept his counsels well, he gave effect to his opinions by passing his Household Suffrage Bill in 1868, afterwards extended to the counties by the joint efforts of Mr. Gladstone and Sir Stafford Northcote at a later date. The late Mr. J. W. Henley, the member for Oxfordshire, may fairly be considered the reviver, if not the author, of household suffrage. In allusion to lowering the household franchise to an eight-pound or six pound rental, he said, "You had better give household suffrage at once, or some day there will be an *ugly rush* to get over the boundary."

With far-seeing policy, Mr. Disraeli followed Mr. Henley's advice; and, although Lord Derby said it was a "leap in the dark," the result has proved what Mr. Disraeli has often said to me, that there is an undercurrent of thorough conservatism amongst the lower strata of the nation, and that "Tory principles are nothing unless popular."

The County contest was between the Marquis of Chandos, only son of the Duke of Buckingham, who was known throughout England as "the Farmers' Friend," on the Tory side; and John Smith, the uncle of the late Lord Carrington, who was then the Hon. Robert Smith, and had resigned his seat for the county to represent his pocket-borough of High Wycombe, on the Reform side, with Pascoe Grenfell as his partner. The Marquis was returned at the head of the poll, polling more plumpers than Smith did votes; if another Tory had been started, the Smith family would have lost the county seat. The bands of music playing all day and a great part of the night; the blaze of many huge flags and banners; the rosettes of the supporters of the various candidates—the green of Lord Chandos, the orange and blue of Smith, the crimson of Mr. Grenfell, with the Borough colours (purple and white) of Rickford, and the crimson and white of Kirkwall, the Grenville green of Lord Nugent and his nephew the Marquis; the shouting of the partisans, who filled the streets in thousands, for nearly eight or ten days; the noise of coaches, post-chaises, and vehicles of every description, passing along the streets—this exciting scene made a deep impression on my boyish mind. My father's house was the head-quarters of the Smiths, but he and all the family remained true to our Tory principles.

Lord Chandos rode into the town on the day of the nomination at the head of at least 700 horsemen, composed of county gentlemen, farmers, and village tradesmen, all well-mounted and wearing green favours on their breasts or laurel in their hats, and preceded by a band of thirty performers—I will not call them musicians, being selected more as voters than for any proficiency in music; about twenty green flags fluttered over the procession bearing suitable mottoes in letters of gold. The equestrians were followed by a train of carriages half a mile in length. Mr. Smith, being an old man, came in a carriage and four, followed by an immense cavalcade with two huge flags emblazoned with the family arms and the motto, *Tenax in fide*. At the head of the Tory procession was a man dressed as a lace-maker in women's clothes, with a lace-making pillow and bobbins complete, emblematic of the Buckinghamshire staple manufacture; and all the green flags had borders nearly two inches wide of beautiful lace, for which a large sum of money was paid. At the conclusion, and after the declaration, of the poll, the chairing took place round all the principal streets in the town, the members, for their personal security, being surrounded by at least a hundred men carrying staves made of handles of hay-forks. The members having alighted at their respective inns, a free fight ensued, heads were cracked, and a scene of trouble and excitement terminated the election.

The Town was not behind the County in the luxurious character of its contest. The Borough of Aylesbury elections were always fought out on the bitterest party lines, and on the days of nomination personalities were freely indulged in. In the year 1802 the Borough consisted only of the parish of Aylesbury. As I have mentioned, it was, in fact, more than household suffrage, and every one who "paid his scot and bore his lot" was a voter. On the occasion of this election the bribery was so outrageous and so openly practised by all three candidates, that a Committee of the House of Commons recommended that the Borough should be thrown open to the Hundreds as well as the Parish of Aylesbury. The candidates were the old sitting members, Mr. Bernard and Mr. Du Pre, who were unexpectedly opposed by a Mr. Bent, a Liverpool merchant and West Indian planter, and a stranger to the town. Soon after his arrival, liveliness took the place of the every-day routine, and for more than three weeks the place was almost a pandemonium. I have heard old people tell tales which would seem incredible had not the facts come out in the main before the Commons Committee. Most of the inns and public-houses were *opened* as it was called, and central committees formed for conducting the election.

The head-quarters of Bernard was the George, Mr.

Du Pre held high festival at the White Hart, and Mr. Bent nailed his colours to the sign of the Bull's Head. Eating and drinking were continuous, and on certain nights in the week each of the agents appeared at head-quarters with a bowl of sparkling punch before him, and another bowl of guineas; the former was ladled out to all who chose to come for it, and those who were thought staunch had from one to five guineas handed to them. It was arranged that these meetings should not clash, and they were held on different nights, so that it was no uncommon thing for a certain number of electors to call at each committee-room and receive the bribe and treating from all three candidates. Innumerable fights took place; and on the day of the nomination one huge orgy prevailed. At the close of the poll, which lasted four days, Du Pre was at the head, Bent next, and Bernard was rejected, much to the chagrin and annoyance of the Grenville and Buckingham party, who had felt quite confident of success.

Bernard subsequently presented a petition against the return of Bent; after a number of irregularities had been proved, Bent waited on Du Pre and said if he did not pay the expenses of his (Bent's) election, he on his part would petition against Du Pre, and the latter, rather than lose his seat, consented to be bled to a fat tune. Thus Bent was unseated, and the Borough was represented by Du Pre and Bernard. As an instance of the extent to which bribery was then carried, it is an amusing fact that it was proved that Bent's people enlisted the choir at the parish church on their side, who, being well paid for their services, gave out and sang at church each Sunday during the contest the 57th Psalm, 5th verse, New Version, " O God, my heart is fixed, '*tis Bent*," the last word being bawled out with great emphasis. After this the Borough was thrown open to the Three Hundreds of Aylesbury, and so continued until the Reform Bill of 1880, when the old Borough was abolished and its boundaries enlarged; it is now called the Aylesbury or Mid-Bucks Division of the County.

I often meet with people who fail to understand the meaning of a Member of Parliament accepting the Stewardship of the "Chiltern Hundreds," the form, of course, by which a member vacates his seat. The Chiltern Hundreds are the Hundreds that cover and abut on the Chiltern Hills, and consist of the Three Hundreds of Aylesbury, the Hundred of Burnham, the Hundred of Stoke, and the Hundred of Desborough. These Hills were mostly covered by beech-trees and thick scrub, and three of the great London roads to the north pass over the hills and through the thick woods, which used to be at one time infested by robbers and dangerous characters, and people journeying to the Metropolis were molested, robbed, and sometimes murdered by lawless gangs. As early as in the days of the Henrys and Edwards, the Crown appointed certain Knights as Stewards of these Hundreds, who had the modest salary of forty shillings a year, that they with their retainers should protect all travellers on their way. It was held more as an office of honour than one of gain, and, as it was a service held under the Crown, any one appointed as one of the Stewards, if he was a Member of Parliament, was obliged to vacate his seat, in the same way as a Solicitor-General and several other members of a Government, who, however, seek re-election. An office of the same character is the Stewardship of the Manor of Worksop.

Although I believe open bribery was destroyed at Aylesbury by enlarging the boundary of the Borough, still treating was carried on to a great extent. And there was some excuse; the Borough became of an unwieldy area, containing parishes and places as much as fifteen miles distant from the town, and as every voter had to be conveyed to the poll at Aylesbury itself, a whole day was often spent by a man in going to and fro. I shall give later some curious details of election expenses to show what long purses elections in the good old times could drain. But it is not only for records of bribery that Aylesbury has a past worth noting: many interesting events are connected with the representation of the Borough.

Sir Henry Austen Layard was first returned to Parliament for Aylesbury in conjunction with Mr. Bethell, who became Lord-Chancellor Westbury. Mr. Layard was subsequently defeated by Mr., afterwards Sir, Thomas Bernard, the son of the Bernard of 1802. We heard many stories of the future Lord-Chancellor whilst he was member for Aylesbury; a marvellous advocate no doubt, he was nevertheless a conspicuous failure in Parliament, and even as a political speaker when addressing his constituents he was extremely disagreeable, a certain mincing manner of delivery did not at all please the rough-and-ready voters of the immaculate Borough

SIR RICHARD BETHELL.

of Aylesbury. When he started for the Borough his great patron was Mr. Acton Tindal, and both he and Bethell were members of the Conservative Club; yet Bethell came forward to oppose Bousfield Ferrand, who was already in the field as the Tory and Protectionist candidate, Bethell posing as the champion of Free Trade and advanced Whiggery. He defeated Ferrand during the last half-hour of the poll by twenty-two votes out of a constituency of 1200.

As this was a test election in an agricultural constituency about Protection and Free Trade, it made the Conservative party extremely angry, and they proposed that both Bethell and Tindal should be expelled from the Conservative Club. At that time Mr. W. Beresford, one of the members for Essex, had made himself very notorious for his pronounced Toryism, and had delivered some very foolish speeches. He was known in the House of Commons by the sobriquet of "W. B." At the meeting to consider the expulsion, as the club-room was crowded, "W. B." got on a chair at the back of the room, and during Bethell's speech in defence of himself, called out, "Speak louder, we can't hear you." Bethell turned round, pointed at "W. B.," and, in his sneering way, said, "Can't you hear me? Why, your ears are long enough." When wit failed him, rudeness was a sure resource. Another story was equally characteristic. It is related that when Bethell was offered the Vice-Chancellorship he said, " I do not see the force of giving up fourteen thousand a year, and the pleasure of making very good speeches, for that of taking five thousand a year and the misery of listening to very bad ones." He once remarked, when he became Solicitor-General, that "he thought the constituency of the Borough of Aylesbury was one of the most poverty-stricken in England, as it was wonderful the number of applications he had from all sorts and conditions of men for situations and places under Government, from commissionerships down to that of village postman; it seemed that so long as it was 'a place,' it did not much matter what the endowment might be."

At one General Election, Messrs. Bernard and Bethell, as the sitting members, intended to offer their services again, when suddenly Mr. C. Vernon Wentworth, a Whig, was started, it was said, to gain the seat from the Tory, Mr. Thos. Bernard; but the Rothschild party, who were the strong supporters of Sir Richard Bethell, thought his seat was in danger, and were determined that Wentworth should be withdrawn. The Conservatives had started Mr. Saml. Geo. Smith, and offered to withdraw their candidate if Mr. Vernon Wentworth was withdrawn, and thus leave the position unchanged; but the Wentworth party refused, the final result being that Sir Richard decamped and hurried off to Wolverhampton, where he was returned, and retained that seat until his elevation to the Woolsack as Baron Westbury. This election was memorable as ending in a tie, Mr. Bernard being returned at the head of the poll by a narrow majority of seven, whilst Mr. Smith and Vernon Wentworth tied. The returning-officers returned all three to Parliament till, after a very expensive scrutiny, Mr. Smith was finally declared elected, and held the seat for twenty-one years, although strongly opposed on two occasions by Mr. Geo. Howell, as a Labour candidate, a man who, although born of no high degree, has proved himself able and honourable, and who conducted both these contests in a very proper manner. Mr. Smith in the end was beaten by Mr. Geo. Erskine Russell, much to the surprise of all his party, who had deemed his seat as safe as an hereditary title.

When Bethell retired it was in the beginning of the month of April, and I had invited Baron Lionel Rothschild to a hunt breakfast at my house, with all those who hunted with him, and to turn out the deer on my farm afterwards. There were a great number present, a brilliant field with many ladies, the day being fine and the sun warm. The stag, after being turned out, took towards Wendover and then up the Chiltern Hills; the pace was severe, and, although only a five-mile point, men and horses were much fatigued. After breasting the hills I returned, and whilst riding home overtook Lord Burghersh, who was one of the hunting party, and like myself was fagged out, and came into my house to have some refreshment. On entering the breakfast-room we found Baron Lionel already seated, refreshing himself with lobster salad, and we began at once to refer to a conversation we had had in the morning about our withdrawing Mr. Smith and the Whigs Mr. Wentworth. Baron Lionel struck the table angrily and said, " Mark my words, if any of my tenants vote for that fellow Wentworth, I'll turn them out of their farms." Lord Burghersh burst out laughing, and, dropping his knife and fork, said, " What! is this the way of the great Liberal member for the City of

London? I thought it was only we old Tories who did this sort of thing!" "I don't care," said the Baron, "if Wentworth stands Bethell shall retire at once"; and he did, for he left the town that night for good. I mention this to show how bitterly the Rothschilds and the landed gentry, Liberal as well as Tory, at that time resented any interference with their power—for a great power this family had become in the neighbourhood of Aylesbury. After this election, Mr. Nathaniel Rothschild, Baron Lionel's eldest son, became the M.P. for Aylesbury, and retained his seat until he was called to the House of Lords as the first peer of the Jewish persuasion that ever entered that august assembly.

While on a visit once at Rotherham in Yorkshire, I heard a curious story of the great Arkwright, the inventor of the marvellous machinery which gained England superiority over the world in the manufacture of cotton, which—I give it *cum grano salis*—illustrates how bribery at elections was not always an unmixed evil. At a General Election, I think in 1784, Mr. Lascelles was one of the candidates for Preston, backed by the interest of the Harewood family. Enormous sums were spent by the candidates on either side. During the polling, which lasted many days, Mr. Lascelles was told that there was a barber named Arkwright, who lived in a cellar and shaved his customers for a penny, who had not voted, and wished to see him. Mr. Lascelles went off alone the next morning and sat down to be shaved. When the operation was completed, he told Mr. Arkwright, the barber, who he was, and gave him a ten-pound Bank of

England note. The barber discovered in a moment the meaning of the gift, thanked him, and said, "Sir Thomas," meaning his opponent, "has been shaved twice this morning!" Mr. Lascelles, going to the glass, rubbed his chin and thoughtfully remarked, "I think you have not done this quite clean, you had better take a little more off," and again sat down in the chair. Arkwright gave him another lathering, and scraped him a little more. When Mr. Lascelles said it would do nicely and produced two more tenners, the barber, slapping his thigh, cried out, "Now, sir, my fortune is made; I wanted fifty pounds, and I have got it." He went off and voted for Lascelles, who was returned by a small majority. Some years afterwards, when Mr. Lascelles had become Earl of Harewood, he was seated in his library at Harewood House, when he saw a brilliant equipage approach, and a gentleman step out of it, who was announced as Mr. Arkwright. His Lordship said he had not the pleasure of knowing him. "Do you remember," was the reply, " being shaved by a man in a very humble position when you were elected for Preston?" "That he remembered well," his lordship answered, "and had often told the singular story." "Well," said Arkwright, "I am that man, and the money you paid me for my services, added to what your adversary gave me, made up fifty pounds. That sum enabled me to bring out my spinning machinery, the foundation of my fortune, and anything in the world I can do for you I will, as I look upon you as the greatest of my benefactors."

During the discussions and decisions of Parliament

on the great Reform Bill of 1832, party spirit ran high, and the Tory and Whig gentry of the period freely bandied about personalities, which, nearly always witty and sharp, were sometimes characterized by the most bitter taunts. In my boyhood, as I have said, I had many opportunities in our old county town of Aylesbury of enjoying the fun of being present on the nomination day of both County and Borough. I have mentioned the contest between "Little David" and the "Giant Goliath," at which, after a five days' poll of the Borough and Hundreds, Lord Kirkwall was defeated, and the two Reform candidates, Lord Nugent and Mr. Rickford, were elected. Lord Nugent was notorious for never paying his tradesmen, and also for being fond of certain members of the fair sex. His residence, The Lilies, was about four miles from the town, and he was often met, as he was riding in to complete his canvass, by young men dressed in women's clothes, and curtseying and ogling him as he passed up the streets; and long imaginary tradesmen's bills, unreceipted, were carried before him and waved triumphantly in his face. These pleasantries generally ended in a row and free fight, the supporters of "Little David" as a rule proving victorious.

The Parliament did not last long, and on its dissolution, after the passing of the Reform Bill, the two sitting members offered themselves for re-election, Mr. Rickford receiving the second votes of both parties. Mr. Winthrop Mackworth Praed, then a young barrister on the Norfolk Circuit, and very popular in Aylesbury, entered the lists against Lord Nugent, nothing daunted by his lordship's former success, nor by his having been member for Aylesbury since the year 1816. Mr. Praed had concluded an exceptionally brilliant career at Oxford, his oratorical powers at the Bar had already attracted attention, and his ever-famous poems received the universal praise of nearly all of his literary contemporaries. His wife—who, I believe, was a West Indian lady, an exceedingly beautiful brunette—canvassed with her husband most effectively. Lord Nugent, as an old Parliamentary hand, made light of the opposition of "the unknown resident," as Mr. Winthrop Praed was called, and taunted him with his want of connection with the ancient Borough of Aylesbury. On the nomination day, on the hustings, one of his lordship's leading supporters called out during Mr. Praed's brilliant address, "Who are you? Where do you come from? Where do you live?" Mr. Praed stopped, and promptly tackled his opponent: "Well, my good fellow, if I am defeated, which you seem confident I shall be, it matters not where I come from or where I live; but if you elect me, which I think you will, why, perhaps at 'The Lilies,' for I hear it is to be let!"

This sally was received with shouts of laughter by the bulk of his hearers, and gave great chagrin to Lord Nugent's supporters, as it had lately leaked out that his lordship, through impecuniosity, could not remain at The Lilies much longer. In the end Mr. Praed was returned after a severe contest, and Lord Nugent, for the first time in his political career, was defeated; the Whig Government, however, shortly after solaced him with the position of Lord High Commissioner of the

Ionian Islands. Winthrop Praed did not live long to enjoy his Parliamentary honours; consumption carried him off in the midst of a promising political and literary career, but his fugitive poems and more ambitious works will long remain to testify to his elegant and refined tastes.

Two hard fights for the honour of representing the Borough afterwards took place between Mr. Thomas Benjamin Hobhouse, of philosophical Radical celebrity, fighting for the Whig-Radical party, and Colonel Hanmer for the Tories. The former, it was said, endeavoured to regain the seat as a warming-pan for Lord Nugent; but in both instances, after a very severe struggle, the Colonel triumphed, and Mr. Hobhouse's philosophical ideas were not aired in the House of Commons. Mr. Rice Clayton, an independent country gentleman, later represented the Borough, and became endeared to all parties by his kindly intercourse with his constituents, especially with the poorer classes. Against him Lord Nugent, on his return, started again as a candidate at the next dissolution. The Conservative party, to retain the second seat, put up a Mr. Dering, an architect and a Royal Academician, but politically an imbecile. Mr. Clayton had given the Duke of Buckingham offence by supporting Sir Robert Peel in his financial policy, and the extreme Tory party quietly and secretly made a compact with the extreme Radicals to run in Lord Nugent, whilst they were to give their second votes to Mr. Dering. The plot succeeded, and, to the surprise and disgust of independent Conservatives, the much-beloved Rice Clayton was defeated. He wrote an admirable and severe letter in *The Times* after the election, showing up in no half-tints the conduct of the Duke of Buckingham and his supporters in voting for the two extremes, and concluded by the prophecy : " My Lord Duke, the day of reckoning will surely come." Sure enough, in a very few months the financial crash of his Grace came, and after a twenty-eight days' sale, the whole of the splendid contents of his palatial residence at Stowe came under the auctioneer's hammer, and the autocratic duke politically ceased to exist.

After returning members to Parliament for over 300 years, the ancient Borough of Aylesbury, the first battle-ground of John Wilkes, was merged into the Division of Mid-Bucks, to be represented by that overpowering monied family, the Rothschilds, yet very popularly so, first by Lord Rothschild and now by Baron Ferdinand.

But before I conclude my sketch of the Parliamentary history of my native borough, I must mention again the election of 1818, when Lord Nugent and Mr. Rickford defeated the Hon. C. C. Cavendish, so that I may give a curious illustration of the manner in which some elections at this period were conducted.

From some old account books in my possession, I find Mr. Cavendish and his friends occupied the White Hart. The committee met in March and continued to sit for three months, and they managed to guzzle and expend no less than £287 2s. 2d. There was also an executive committee, who professed to assist the other, and their little bill amounted to £108 4s. 6d.; but the really harrowing part of the business for this losing candidate must have been that of paying the bill for the necessary refreshments of the loyal and independent voters who had failed to return him. As a curiosity, I append the bill verbatim. The first day it will be perceived that there were as follows—

	£	s	d.
1818. 1st Day's Poll.			
June 24.—25 Breakfasts—Solicitors, Clerks, etc.	1	17	6
40 Freeholders' do.	3	0	0
384 do. Dinners	58	12	0
52 do. Solicitors, Clerks, etc.	13	0	0
Beer	15	0	0
Wine	130	0	0
Rum, Brandy, etc.	6	0	0
50 Stavesmen, Breakfasts, Dinners, Suppers, and Beer	16	5	0
	£243	14	6
2nd day's poll, as before (but only 230 voters dined)	176	5	0
3rd day's poll (120 voters dined)	95	5	6
4th day's poll (25 voters dined)	30	12	0
Total	£545	17	0

There were therefore 759 voters entertained in the four days, although only 420 voted, so the cost came to about 26s. per head.

There was also a bill for the day of the declaration of the poll and the chairing, which amounted to £56 13s., and for posting and baiting of horses, £105 8s. 8d.; so that the committee and a few extras brought the total up to £1,101 9s. 3d. This sum was paid without a murmur, and a compliment to the proprietor of the inn on the great moderation of his account. From the old books I also extract the bill of fare of one day's dinner, and it will be seen that a substantiality pervaded everything—20 dishes fish ; 10 dishes boiled fowls ; 10 ditto roast ditto ; 1 ditto boiled leg pork and peas-pudding ; 2 ditto hams ; 2 ditto haunches of mutton ; 6 ditto geese ; 10 ditto pigeon-pies ; 3 ditto boiled beef ; 3 ditto roast ditto ; 2 ditto fillets veal ; 1 ditto loin ditto ; 1 ditto roast leg pork ; 2 ditto forequarters ditto ; 1 roast turkey ; 1 boiled ditto ; 2 roast pigs ; 16 plum-puddings ; 60 custard ditto ; 20 fruit-pies ; 10 dishes custard ; fruit ditto, ditto ; blanc-mange, jellies, etc. etc. Well may the loyal and independent voters regret the loss of the "good old times !"

Some very amusing stories are told about the feasting that went on at several of the lesser inns ; but one bill sent in was so outrageous in the charges, that the committee were determined to examine the premises, and when they had measured up the cubical contents of the cellar, they found that if it had been filled from the floor to the ceiling and close up to the door, it would not contain much more than half the wine, spirits, and beer charged for. The landlord of this hostelry sat comfortably smoking his pipe in the parlour when the agents of the Hon. C. C. Cavendish came into the house to settle the bill, and Boniface, not daring to meet them, left it to his wife to complete the bargain. The only accounts which could be furnished were sundry chalk marks on the backs of doors of the rooms wherein the voters had been entertained ; under the head of "Beer" were a great number of lines, showing how many quarts of that potent beverage had been there consumed, also innumerable strokes of chalk for the tumblers of grog and punch, and, in addition, like marks for every bottle of strong port and fiery sherry, concluding with a line to indicate the numbers who had breakfasted and dined in each room. So many *doors* had been charged in the bill, at an average of something like £10 to £14 per door; and the good dame was constantly backwards and forwards from her husband to the agents conducting the negotiations. At last the landlord said, with a view of settling the matter—" Very well, then, give 'em a door into the bargain." In the end they deducted a door and a half, and so squared the bill. I am not able to say how much this election cost; but the Hon. Charles left the place, the races were abandoned, and it was many years before any of the family came into the town, and not until about the year 1853 did Mr. Cavendish essay to enter Parliament for his neighbourhood, when he started for the County of Bucks, and was returned as the County representative, with the late Earl of Beaconsfield and Mr. Caledon George Du Pre as his colleagues, and he represented the County until he was created the first Lord Chesham.

The ancient Borough of Agmondesham, previous to the Reform Bill of 1832, returned two members to Parliament, and the family of the Drakes, owning the greater part of the property in the borough, either sat for it themselves or returned whoever they pleased. When I was a boy I remember being present at one of the Amersham elections, and was highly delighted at the fun and the frolic. The candidates stood in front of the old Market Hall on two large stones, and after the usual nomination, in very brief speeches returned thanks for their selection. They then entered their carriages, drawn by four horses, and perambulated the town, followed by a crowd of men, women, and children shouting and dancing around. There was a very curious custom here which I had never heard of at any other town. At each of the inns in the town, and there were only a few, the women-folk, old and young, married and single, assembled — the two best inns being selected by the lady inhabitants, the others according to their order or grade in society—and, being seated round the public room in the house, these fair ones awaited the arrival of the newly-elected Members, who formally entered the room and very deliberately and demurely kissed them in turn. This performance concluded, a raid was made into the inn-rooms by the young men of the place, and, amidst loud laughter and screams and struggles innumerable, they also kissed the not unwilling dames.

It is useless defending the retainers of "rotten boroughs," as they were called; but I cannot forbear mentioning that for strictly honourable, independent conduct, it was well known that none were more entirely unbiassed by political parties than the Members for Amersham, and probably, indeed no doubt, other members for so-called rotten boroughs possessed the same characteristics.

CHAPTER III.

Disraeli's Early Political History—His Election Contest at High Wycombe and an Old Radical Diary—The Story of his Early Radicalism—His Chartist Speech and Repartees on the Hustings—His Noisy Reception at Aylesbury—His Agricultural Foibles—Fawcett, the Comedian—Disraeli on Bob Lowe—His Famous Breakdown—His Boyish Prophecy.

A GREAT deal has been said on many occasions, and as often as not used to the detriment of Lord Beaconsfield, that he was guilty of tergiversation, that he shifted his opinions to suit his own purposes. His opponents and detractors are never satisfied without stating that he commenced his political life as a Radical, and a very advanced one, and that it was only at a later date, after his first public appearance, that he came out as a Tory and a supporter of Tory principles. I am old enough to remember his first appearance, or, at all events, one of his first appearances, as a public speaker, and this was when I was a school-boy, in the year 1832; I well remember his getting up in the County Hall, at the memorable election at that time, which was called the Reform Election. He was then the bitter opponent of the Reform Party, represented by Mr. John Smith, the cousin of the first Lord Carrington, and Mr. Pascoe Grenfell, who were opposed by the champion of the

Tories, the Marquis of Chandos, on whose behalf Mr. Benjamin Disraeli addressed the freeholders. I can see him now as a consummate dandy, in a frock-coat well thrown back, to display a white waistcoat, his hair falling over his shoulders in long black curls which he constantly shook from his face, as he gave vent to his pent-up thoughts. He made a most violent onslaught on the Whigs, which called up to the Council table in the County Hall Mr. Martin Smith, who gave Disraeli's statement the lie direct, and, I believe, challenged him to fight a duel.

Mr. Disraeli's manner was very eccentric, and he was laughed at as a mountebank and a Jew adventurer; even his own—the Tory—party gave him the cold shoulder; but he persevered, and at last made his speech, through the storm of ridicule and roars of laughter which greeted his singular antics.

I have before me a copy of an old diary written by a well-known Reformer or Radical in 1832, and find in it the following—

"Wycombe Election.

"June 3.—E. Lytton Bulwer writes to B. Disraeli, Esq.: 'Mr. Hume expresses his great satisfaction in hearing that you were about to start for Wycombe. He has a high opinion of your talent and principles.' D. O'Connell writes to Lytton Bulwer: 'I have no acquaintance to whom I could recommend Mr. Disraeli. It grieves me, therefore, to be unable to serve him on his canvass.' Sir Francis Burdett also writes to Charles Gore: 'I am sorry I have not it in my power to promote Mr. Disraeli's return to Parliament.' Jos. Hume also writes in a similar strain. What a Radical this Disraeli must be to be found in such company.

"4.—The Reform Bill passes the House of Lords.

"7.—The Reform Bill receives the Royal Assent.

"9.—Colonel Grey, son of the Premier, appears as a candidate for Wycombe in the place of Sir Thos. Baring, who has resigned. The Colonel made a hasty but a very successful canvass.

"12.—Colonel Grey's address to the electors of Wycombe is published.

"13.—Mr. Disraeli makes a public entry into Wycombe, standing in an open carriage drawn by four horses; a great concourse went out to The Bird in Hand to meet him, and there were music and banners. Mr. Disraeli addressed the populace from the portico of the Lion Hotel.

"26th was Wycombe Election, and there was great excitement. The contest was between Colonel Grey and Mr. Disraeli; the nomination was first private in the Council Chamber, and afterwards in public, although the public had no voice in the matter. Mr. Disraeli was proposed by Sprowster and King, and Colonel Grey by Wheeler and Rumsey. Both candidates addressed the assembly amidst great uproar. Polling commenced, and at five o'clock Disraeli retired, the numbers being—

Grey	23
Disraeli	12
Majority for Grey	11

"Mr. Disraeli made an angry speech after the poll closed; Grey was chaired."

"What a different constituency to ours," the writer goes on to say, referring to Aylesbury. "Here every man who boils his own pot has a vote. (This is the meaning of a pot-waller.) At Wycombe the Corporation returns the members; this, however, is the last election under the old style; the next will be on the popular system of representation."

The Reform Bill received the Royal Assent on June 7th, and on the following December 3rd, Parliament was dissolved; on the 10th the election for High Wycombe took place under the new franchise. The candidates were the Hon. Robert Smith and Colonel Grey on the side of the then Whig Government, and Mr. Disraeli as their opponent in the Tory interest. He was proposed by a leading Tory of the town, and seconded by a Radical, as the extreme party were very bitter against the Whigs, Dan O'Connell at that time calling them "The base, bloody, and brutal Whigs." Disraeli had the show of hands with Smith, and Grey demanded a poll.

On December 11th, the first day, at the close of the poll, the numbers were—

Smith	171
Grey	136
Disraeli	107

12th.—The second day, at the final close of poll, it was—

Smith	179
Grey	140
Disraeli	119

It will be seen that Smith only increased his poll the second day by eight votes and Grey by but four votes, whereas Mr. Disraeli had polled twelve votes more than the first day. I have not been able to find out how many voters remained unpolled, but so small a majority over Disraeli shows how fully justified he was in fighting his battle.

I now come to the serious charge, reiterated over and over again, that he commenced his political career as a Radical, backed up by the strong recommendations of the leaders of the extreme party, and that he distinctly advocated their opinions. I find that he did support the vote by ballot, and an enlargement of the franchise, which was not to be wondered at when he was rejected so decisively by the close Corporation of High Wycombe, and that even when the borough was said to be thrown open, the whole place was merely an appanage of the House of Smith, for each attempt to wrest the borough from the Carrington family proved it to be as rotten a family borough as any in the kingdom. But the facts of the case were told me a few years since by a clergyman, a man of the highest character, who, I know from his position, was able to corroborate every particular, and they were so singular and cogent, that I unhesitatingly place in this account my sincere belief.

He told me that at that time, December, 1832, he was an undergraduate at Oxford; that he was most intimately acquainted with Benjamin Disraeli as young men together; and that he was fired with the political enthusiasm of the young, and came up from Oxford to render his friend all the assistance in his power, to canvass for him, and endeavour to carry his election. A few days before the election, a party delegation of about twenty-five electors came to Mr. Disraeli's committee-room and stated that they—as representing the extreme Radicals—were so disgusted at the treatment that their party were receiving from the Whig Government, that, if Mr. Disraeli could get any letters of introduction from their leaders, they would join the Tory party and vote for him; and moved also by his own animosity to the Whig oligarchy, Mr. Disraeli undertook, through some friends of his, to get a letter from both Mr. Daniel O'Connell and Mr. Hume, who wrote and recommended their friends at Wycombe to support his candidature. Now comes a remarkable coincidence. Old Mr. Norris, the then owner of Hughenden Manor, was one of Disraeli's staunchest supporters; he had known him from boyhood, his house being only an easy walk from Bradenham, the residence of Mr. Disraeli's father. He had invited Disraeli to luncheon on the day before the election, and in the meantime Mr. Disraeli's committee had received these two letters from Messrs. Hume and O'Connell, printed and circulated them throughout the borough, and a copy had got into Mr. Norris's hands, which so roused his indignation that he determined to forbid the young candidate the house on his arrival to luncheon. When Mr. Disraeli arrived he met him at the door, refused him admittance, and shut the door in his face. Mr. Disraeli lived to see the day when through that very door he welcomed the Queen of England to visit him as his guest.

My readers will allow that so strange and eventful a circumstance is worth recording, and doubtless had some influence at a later day, when his circumstances were more prosperous, in the Premier's desire to purchase Hughenden Manor.

It will be seen by these statements that Mr. Disraeli's opinions were more formed by the fact of his hatred to Whiggery, which pervades all his early novels, than by a belief in the extreme doctrines of Radicalism.

I remember once when visiting at Hughenden, that Mr. Disraeli put on his billy-cock hat, and with his legs enclosed in leather gaiters and a spud in his hand, he suggested taking a walk through that portion of the beech-woods surrounding the north-west of the Manor House, which he called the "German forest." We were talking on many subjects, and as we passed an opening in the woods, he said, "Come here, and sit ye down," and he led the way to a rough seat made of some split larch fir-poles, and completely out of sight of the "madding crowd." He remarked, "This is a favourite resort of mine. You can see no trace of a human being. I have only the beech-woods, primroses, and wild-flowers about me, and, more than all, it shuts out any view of Wycombe"—and he smiled complacently, and talked of farming, and the future prospects of that business. I spoke, amongst other real or imaginary grievances, about the incidence of the Game Laws as injuring the work of improvement on the land, and he said, "I would soon settle that question; a very short Act of Parliament should be passed, which would be, in my opinion, effectual." I ventured to ask what it was, and he replied, "Abolish gamekeepers." To this I cordially assented, and said they were never contented until they had set the landlord against the tenants, making mischief between them in every way—that this did not apply to all, but no tenant of gentlemanly feeling would submit to the tyranny of these generally ignorant men. He then said, "I have down in the autumn my friends, Lords Derby, Exeter, and Salisbury, and others, and they tell me they get as good sport at Hughenden as they do anywhere. My tenants are my gamekeepers; they vie with each other in keeping up a good head of game; my larder is generally well filled, and it costs me nothing."

I can fully endorse these opinions. When Mr. Cresswell Baker owned the parish of Hulcot, near Aylesbury—now the property of the Rothschild family—he acted in the same manner by his tenants; he came down with his friends a little before Michaelmas, held his rent-audit, and I have heard many a good-natured quarrel over the dinner-table as to the number of coveys of birds on each tenant's farm, and as to who could show most hares and rabbits also.

On one occasion, in conversation with Disraeli on some of his speeches and opinions in Parliament, he made a very curious but truthful remark, which should be recorded. It may be thought too severe; but I, who knew how he had been shunted and traduced, with the cold shoulder given to him on many occasions in his early career by the county squires, was not surprised at the sarcasm.

I was mentioning that he once made a speech some

years since, when speaking of the Fergus O'Connor Chartist gatherings; that the report in the papers stated that he turned round towards his own party, and said, "Why do the people elect leaders from amongst themselves? Because you, the country gentlemen of England, neglect them. If you were to do as you did of old, place yourselves at their head, they would blindly, gladly follow you." These were something like the words I reminded him of, and he looked at me and said, "Yes, Mr. Fowler, and if they don't do that, of what use are country gentlemen?" As Artemus Ward says: "The rebook was severe but merited."

Many a time I have heard the great Minister crush his democratic opponents by some severe but good-humoured remark which brought on the speaker the ridicule of even his own friends and supporters. His readiness of retort, his imperturbable gravity, the twinkle of his eye, his apparently suppressed laughter at his own remarks, were irresistible. A Mr. Barry, of Chilton, a prominent Radical Dissenter, never let an occasion pass that he did not ask him if he would vote for the abolition of Church-rates. He listened patiently to his question, and said, "On so many occasions this gentleman has asked the self-same question, that if I wanted another reason to those he had already given, it would be that if Church-rates were abolished, 'Othello's occupation would be gone.'" On another nomination day he was speaking very deliberately and calmly on some great foreign question, when a man in the crowd sang out, "Speak louder and quicker." He stopped, singled the man out at once, and, pointing his finger at him, spoke very slowly and said, "I am obliged to speak slowly to drive what I have to say into your thick head." "You've got it now, Joe," said the fellow's companions, and silence reigned immediately.

The County Election took place in December, 1832, the candidates being the Marquis of Chandos and Mr. Scott Murray (Tories), Mr. John Smith and Mr. Dashwood (Whigs); and at the nomination in the County Hall at Aylesbury, after the candidates had been nominated, the local paper says—"Mr. D'Israeli now presented himself, and there at once occurred an uproar of the most extravagant description. Some half-dozen of the virulent Tories, including the 'petty officials,' and not excluding the Under-Sheriff (Mr. Tindal), seemed to be disposed to support him, but all the Tories of a higher class joined the great bulk of the meeting in their determination to resist his attempt to gain a hearing. He assumed several of his best attitudes and executed his lungs to the utmost, but to no purpose, except that every fresh effort he made produced additional groans, and a volley of such epithets as 'Tory Radical,' 'Radical Tory,' 'Mountebank Orator,' etc., etc. Some made an objection to him that he was not a freeholder. He declared he was, but not registered. It was then contended, amidst the storm, that, not being registered, he had no right to speak. A great uproar ensued," of which I, although a boy, was an eye-witness, and can vouch for its truth; and the report goes on to state—"Mr. D'Israeli" (at that time this was the way his name was spelt) "again stood forward and exerted his voice to the utmost. He appeared to be in great anger, and was most violent in his action. At last, directing his observations to a particular part of the meeting, first pointing his finger, and then doubling his fist, he was just heard to say, 'Those gentlemen, so safe, so circumspect, and so cowardly——' The words were no sooner uttered than Mr. John Abel Smith, son of Mr. John Smith, one of the candidates, rushed forward, and springing on the table, apparently under the influence of strong indignation, went up to Mr. D'Israeli, whom he called on instantly to disclaim the expressions so addressed to him. This we understood Mr. D'Israeli to do. Mr. D'Israeli professed himself ready to explain, if the meeting would give him a hearing. The interest felt in the proceeding just witnessed procured for him at last that for which he had been so long labouring in vain. He said that as regarded what had just transpired, if, in the heat of the moment, excited as he naturally was, he had uttered anything that had wounded the feelings of any gentleman, he was sorry for it. (Cheers.) Mr. D'Israeli, having thus got the ear of the meeting, indulged himself, as usual, in abusing the Whigs. He was much interrupted."

The result of the poll was—

Chandos (T.) ...	2856
Smith (W.) ...	2402
Dashwood (W). ...	1646
Scott Murray (T.)	1534

I have quoted rather largely from this local paper, which at that time was the only one in the county, but was a strong Whig journal, for it shows how baseless is the charge that at the outset of his career he came forward as a Radical. In allusion to his defeat at High Wycombe, this same paper says—" The die is cast. The Bradenham braggart is rejected, and the electors of Wycombe have to congratulate themselves on the glorious termination of a glorious struggle, and the Hon. Colonel Grey has been elected. It must be admitted that Mr. D'Israeli's manner is imposing, his voice powerful, and his action extraordinary; but the electors of Wycombe rejoice that he has bade them adieu—to him they say, 'Farewell for ever.'"

Lord Beaconsfield—whilst Mr. Disraeli, as M.P. for Bucks—was always particularly anxious to pose as the British farmer, and phrases in many of his speeches have become household words. In one of his after-dinner speeches, at which I was present, he had a chance to show off his agricultural knowledge, and in speaking of the advantages of farmers breeding their own stock, he told them, as a great piece of original discovery in sheep-breeding, " that they should cross their Downs with Cotswolds." As this had been the practice for many years with nearly three-fourths of his hearers, there was not much valuable information in the advice; but our facetious contemporary, Mr. *Punch*, seized upon the phrase, and recommended him to cross his party with a dash of his bitterest opponents. On another occasion, in the autumn, which was the time when the agricultural meetings were held, there had been a great drought, and the farmers were bitterly complaining about the shortness of food for their cattle;

Disraeli told them, "from inquiries he had made, that there was not much to complain of"; as although "they had had a poor crop of hay, yet they had an excellent crop of a good juicy root." This startled his hearers, as, from the great drought, the few turnips there were, instead of being juicy, were small and as hard as stones, with no nutriment whatever in them.

This reminds me of a good anecdote which Mr. Vernon, who left his noble gallery of pictures to the nation, used to relate of Fawcett, the comedian, who was often a guest at his house. Fawcett was very desirous of being considered a country gentleman, and took a small place with a little land down in the country, where he found it was the custom of the farmers to assemble and smoke their pipes in the village inn in the evening. He joined them and listened attentively to their conversation. There had been a succession of wet weeks, and one after the other, as they came into the parlour and began filling their pipes, the farmers invariably made the general remark, "Rare weather for turmuts!" which was acquiesced in by the remainder of the party. Fawcett treasured up this remark, and when he got back to London he thought he must show off his agricultural knowledge; and when his friends at the theatre, or anywhere else, were complaining of the wet weather, he always came out as an oracle with the remark, "Rare weather for turnips!" and this phrase obtained him the reputation of being a distinguished authority on farming. It so happened that before he went back again to his country home a very serious drought had set in, and the soil was parched up in all directions; but on his arrival home, as usual, he resorted to his village haunt, and, after the usual greeting, he thought he must show his friends that he had not forgotten their agricultural remarks, and said, "Rare weather for turmuts!" Whereupon the farmers all sprang from their seats as though a bombshell had been thrown amongst them; and one of them shouted out, "D—n it, sir, there ain't a turmut in the country; they be all roasted up." Fawcett rarely ventured again to air his agricultural knowledge.

In addition to Lord Beaconsfield's desire to be an authority on agricultural matters, he was anxious to also pose as a farmer—in full costume. At one of the annual meetings of the Royal and Central Bucks Association, at Aylesbury, those attending the show-yard were startled by the appearance of their beloved M.P. entering in full panoply of agricultural mail, or, as he thought, in full farming costume. He had discarded the traditional top-boots, but appeared in a brown velveteen shooting-coat, with a flapping waistcoat, and over his black trousers he had drawn a pair of long dark-brown leather gaiters, with wooden buttons covered with leather up the side, reaching from his dandy Wellington boots to his hips, and fastened there with leathern straps to his brace buttons; his head was covered with a black "billycock" hat, and a blue bird's-eye silk handkerchief was tied loosely round his neck, and he carried a big stick with a spud at the end; in fact, he looked like a well-dressed gamekeeper. Every one was screaming with laughter, but he thought he was paying us agricultural folk a compliment by wearing what he considered to be the typical dress of the British farmer —he must have been surprised to find many of the real article dressed in the best mo lern style, and several with coats by the well-known Mr. Poole, of Savile Row. These little idiosyncrasies of his rather showed in reality how much he wished to identify himself with his own country people. His speeches at these meetings were half political, and half social and agricultural, and were as well scrutinized by the Press the next day as a Ministerial speech at a Ninth of November Lord Mayor's dinner. One of his most effective hits was made at a political dinner at Newport Pagnell, where he attacked Mr. Bob Lowe (Lord Sherbrooke), who had made a severe harangue against him the previous week. He spoke something like these words: " I now come to the right hon. member for the University of London. Why, this gentleman entirely owes his seat in the House to me! For you may remember that he dared not show his face to any constituency of working-men in the kingdom, for he would assuredly be kicked off any hustings, as he was at Kidderminster; and when we were completing our Reform Bill, we said, What is to be done with the member for Kidderminster? And at last the thought struck me, so that he would not have to face a crowd of voters, we would give a member to the London University, and this would suit him. You may now ask me why we were so anxious to keep the right hon. gentleman in the House? Well, for this reason. We knew that no Liberal Ministry could be complete without Mr. Lowe, and we knew perfectly well that any Ministry of which he formed a part he would inevitably wreck." It is impossible to describe the effect of this climax, as his hearers were wondering, as they intently listened, what explanation he could give for his anxiety to find him a Parliamentary seat.

There have been several versions of his great breakdown, the failure of his first speech in Parliament. One of the reporters of *The Times*, who was present in the House of Commons at the time, told me what he vouched to be the true version. He had begun his speech in a mock heroic style, and alluded to the departure of a beloved monarch,—meaning the death of William IV.,—and the House, which was the first Parliament of Queen Victoria, and for which I think he was returned the first time for Maidstone, began to titter. He then got angry, and his audience bursting out into loud laughter, he turned savagely on them, and said, " You won't hear me now; but the day will come when you shall hear me." He was a *protégé* of Lord Lyndhurst, and there is no doubt that on his first entering into public life he was rather bombastic. When he tried for the borough of Taunton, and was defeated, he said, " Recollect, the author of *Vivian Grey* cannot remain long out of Parliament." This, at the time considered vain and conceited, was only giving voice to the feeling of natural self-consciousness which he possessed in an eminent degree; and after all it is no more than what has been recorded of Sheridan, after his equally conspicuous failure in the House at the commencement of his afterwards brilliant career. He was found in the dining-room of the House of Commons, with his face buried in his hands, and his friend said, " Cheer up, cheer up; others have failed before now;" and he replied, " I know I have got it in me, and, by God, some day it shall come out." There is also the well-known story of Lord Nelson, when commander of the *Captain* at the Battle of St. Vincent, which was fought under Admiral Jervis, Lord St. Vincent. One of Nelson's friends condoled with him on his name being unfairly left out of the despatch, when Nelson had done more than any other commander to win that great battle. "Never mind," was the reply, "I'll have a Gazette of my own some day." It recalls also the celebrated remark on another occasion, "A peerage or Westminster Abbey." Yet Sheridan and Nelson are not accused of conceit.

I was once very intimate with a Mr. Venables, now long passed away, who was a near relative of Alderman Venables, of the City of London, the proprietor of large paper-mills in the neighbourhood of High Wycombe. He told me a most interesting anecdote of the early life of Benjamin Disraeli. When they were boys they often walked home together towards Bradenham, where the elder Disraeli resided. One moonlight night, Benjamin, who, like himself, was about fourteen years of age, was unusually taciturn, walking moodily along, when Venables asked him what he was thinking about. "He answered, very slowly and deliberately, 'I am considering what I shall be. I mean to get myself talked about.' 'How are you going to do that?' said I. 'Well, I shall write a book; then I shall make some speeches, and get into Parliament.' I laughed at him; and he then said, 'And I won't rest till I am made a Privy Councillor.'" "I then told him," said Venables, "not to talk such nonsense as that."

CHAPTER IV.

Bulgarian Atrocities in Buckinghamshire — Lord Beaconsfield's Speech in the Corn Exchange at Aylesbury and Rothschild's Opinion of it—Disraeli and the Cattle Defence Association—Disraeli and Protection—At Hughenden: its Cedars, its Purchase—Mrs. Disraeli's Frugality — The Romantic Story of Miss Williams' Legacy—Disraeli as Chancellor of the Exchequer—His Manchester Speech - His Opinion of the Disfranchising Act of 1832—His Sympathy for the Agricultural Labouring Class: their Earnings, their Right of Combination—On Publicans and Exhausted Volcanoes— His Death and Funeral.

AT the annual meeting of the Royal and Central Buckingham Agricultural Society in 1880, Mr. Disraeli had promised, as was generally his custom, to attend. But he had lately been created Earl of Beaconsfield after his successful completion of the Berl'n Treaty, and his elevation to the peerage had created a vacancy in the representation of the County of Bucks. At this time Mr. Gladstone and others had been stumping the country, haranguing the masses on the so-called " Bulgarian Atrocities " ; the minds of the people were much inflamed, and doubts were entertained if the seat, thus vacated, could be held by the Conservative party, and the bye-election was looked forward to by both sides as a test election of the opinions of the people on this great question. The candidates for the vacant seat were the

Hon. T. Fremantle, eldest son of the late Lord Cottesloe, on the Conservative side, and the Hon. Rupert Carrington, brother of the popular Lord Carrington; and both parties felt confident of success. It need not be said that Lord Beaconsfield looked with the keenest interest on the result of the contest. The polling was fixed for the day after the public dinner of the Agricultural Society, and great anxiety was expressed lest Lord Beaconsfield should be absent from the dinner. A few days before the meeting I had the honour to receive the following letter from Lord Beaconsfield, which I insert from, I hope, a pardonable pride, that my opinion should have been deemed of service to him.

"10, Downing Street, Whitehall,
"*September* 9, 1876.
"DEAR MR. FOWLER,
"You are one of those men in whose judgment and trustworthiness I have great confidence. I should therefore feel obliged to you if you would give me your opinion as to the prospect of our County contest.
"Yours sincerely,
"BEACONSFIELD."

I replied that I felt sure of a successful result, although we were confronted by a very strong opponent, and the representative of one of the most popular families in the county; "but," I concluded my letter, "I feel convinced that your lordship's presence at the dinner will make at least three hundred votes difference to our party."

I heard afterwards that my view was supported by that prince of good fellows, "Squire Drake," of Shardeloes, who wrote to the same effect, and even rode over to Hughenden to persuade the Prime Minister to attend. The Earl then intimated that he would be present and dine with us. I was one of the Dinner Committee, and in forming the list of toasts his name was put down to respond to the "House of Lords." The Committee deputed me on his arrival to wait on him and inform him of the arrangement. His lordship did not appear till late in the afternoon, and, on his arrival at the George, together with the late Sir Robert Harvey, his brother representative in the county, we waited on him, and informed him on what he had to speak, and I shall not forget the annoyance he expressed at it. "What!" he said, "how can they expect me to do this, when I have not taken the oaths nor my seat in the House of Lords yet? Lord Cottesloe should do it— I can't, I can't"; and he hinted that he should go back to Hughenden.

The late Sir Philip Rose, who was present, calling me aside, said, seeing how much vexed his lordship was, that there should be a special toast of "The Prime Minister," and that I must go back to the Committee and arrange it with them. The alteration being cordially accepted by them, I returned and informed Lord Beaconsfield of it, and he was satisfied.

The crowd in and about the George Hotel was very great. The people assembled in the streets to cheer their late Member, and the Corn Exchange, where the dinner was held under the chairmanship of the president of the Society, Mr. Nathaniel Grace Lambert, the Liberal Member of the county, was already crowded, the tables having been laid for five hundred, and the galleries filled with more than four hundred ladies. The Exchange stands at the bottom of the hill in the Market Square, and it was intended that his lordship should walk down, but when he came out of the hotel his carriage was standing to take him there, the servants thinking the crowd would be too great for their master to go through on foot. So he got into the brougham, and, turning round to me, he said, "I must not go alone; you must come with me." As we were going down the Square, he said, "Do they expect me to say anything to-day?" meaning politically, and I replied, "Certainly; we are all looking forward to what you have to say about the Bulgarian atrocities." "I cannot touch upon that; you know how strictly forbidden we are by our Society's rules to speak on political questions." I answered, "Yes; but this is not a political, but a great National Question, and we shall give you such a reception as you never before received in this county." "Do you think so?" he said. "But you know I can't, I must not do it." I then replied, "I think, my lord, I can take a liberty with you. What do you think the public will say if you don't speak on this all-important question?" "What's that?" he said. "Why, that you are afraid of it." He waited a moment and then folded his arms and leant back in the corner of the carriage, and then said, "If that's the case, I will speak."

We then arrived amidst the cheering of the crowd, which was so dense at the entrance to the Corn Exchange that we found it impossible to force our way through into the hall. I then suggested he should enter by my business office, which adjoined, and get in through a back entrance, which led into the building. On arriving there we found the door locked, and all our knocking and banging proved ineffectual to gain admission, the waiters and assistants inside having been strictly ordered not to admit any one that way. In vain I told them it was Lord Beaconsfield, and that we must get in. They only laughed and said, "That won't do for us—that's no Lord Beaconsfield," and thought it was some attempt by people to use his name to obtain admittance. I then told them to go and fetch the Secretary, Mr. Geo. Fell, but nothing would persuade the senseless blockheads to do so.

In the meantime his lordship sat down and waited patiently. When Mr. Denson, the Superintendent of the Police, came to us we again thundered for admission, but without avail. At last Lord Beaconsfield turned round, and with a sly twinkle in his eye, said, "Have you got no experienced burglar about here?" Denson replied, "If I had authority, my lord, I'd soon get admission." "Well," I said, "I will give you that, as I am one of the Directors of the Market Company;" and he then went into the Butchers' Market, and returning with a large iron meat-hook, wrenched the lock off the door, and in that way the Prime Minister of England entered the hall to make his great speech.

Never shall I forget the scene we encountered as I walked through the hall to conduct him to his seat next the Chairman. The whole audience rose; the cheering and clapping of hands, the waving of handkerchiefs from the ladies in the gallery, continued for several minutes; his political opponents caught the contagion and seemed to vie with his supporters in the ovation. After dinner and the usual preliminary toasts had been disposed of, my old friend, John Treadwell, a typical British farmer, rose and proposed the "Prime Minister," and in a few appropriate and well-chosen words gave the toast and the time for three hearty cheers, which were responded to till the iron ribs of the roof reverberated. I need not say with what calmness the Prime Minister spoke, with what earnestness he denounced the false and calumnious charges brought against our allies, how he showed up the specious pretences of the Russians, and how he shattered to pieces the arguments of Mr. Gladstone and his Russian friends. The speech electrified his audience, and the result of the election the next day proved my assertion that his presence at the meeting would make 300 votes difference to our side at the poll, for Mr. Fremantle was returned, to the great surprise of the Liberal party, by a majority of 187. Lord Carrington very freely laid out his money on the occasion of counting the votes after the poll, by laying the odds of three to one on his brother, and losing £50 to Squire Drake.

As a sequel to this political episode, I cannot omit the following incident. About a fortnight after this meeting, an agricultural dinner was held at Princes Risborough, a small town within the district of the Borough of Aylesbury, and one of its polling places, although nine miles from the actual town of Aylesbury. I was walking from the station in company with Sir Nathaniel, now Lord Rothschild, and with him was a leading Liberal Dissenter, who was Chairman of his Committee. Sir Nathaniel remarked, in reference to Lord Beaconsfield's Bulgarian speech, that it was but seldom he made a mistake in public speaking, but that in this instance he made a very great and important one. On my asking what it was, he said, " I was not present ; but I read the report of the speech in *The Times* the next morning, in which he said, ' We are aware that on this question we, the Ministry, are not in accord with the views of the majority in the kingdom.' This was a serious statement, and fraught with serious consequences ;" to which Sir Nathaniel's great supporter said, " Well, but it was quite true." " No," said Sir Nathaniel, " it was not true ; it is only the voice of a noisy minority, who chatter about the country without contradiction, and make out that they are the spokesmen for the nation. Now," he continued, " see the effect of this statement : I happen to know that these words were brought to the attention of the Czar and his ministers, and have encouraged him in his Eastern policy, and proved a great trouble to the English Ministry and their Turkish allies."

I hope my readers will pardon this rather lengthy account of Lord Beaconsfield's first public appearance in the County after he had ceased to represent it in the House of Commons, but it is my greatest pride that I had the distinguished honour to have nominated him as a candidate on the last two occasions on which he stood for the County of Buckingham, and even the details of Disraeli's career are to me, and I think to many besides myself, of peculiar charm and interest.

Soon after he became Earl of Beaconsfield, after his return from his brilliant mission to Berlin, he was at Aylesbury, and on seeing him I remarked he was looking very well. "Yes," he replied, "I am glad to say I am, except for a slight attack of gout;" to which I answered, "But people say if you have an attack of that malady you take a fresh lease of your life." He said, "Well, I am not sure that I would not rather be a tenant-at-will and give up the lease." This remark was in pleasant reference to the many interviews I had had with him on the Agricultural Holdings Act, especially as to tenants-at-will and leaseholders. It was a trait in his character that he invariably consulted those of his constituents who were tolerably well informed on such subjects as required his attention in Parliament, and always availed himself of their practical knowledge in any department which bore upon the subject under discussion.

I had been appointed many years ago Chairman of the "Home Cattle Defence Association," a society which had its centre in London, for pressing on the Government the necessity for stamping out cattle diseases, which are chiefly imported from abroad. This was a subject in which Disraeli expressed considerable interest, and he brought his mind to bear on such details as were necessary to frame such a Bill before Parliament as to ensure its successful career through the House of Commons. One day, when attending Quarter Sessions at Aylesbury, he asked me to come up to Hughenden and to bring with me three others well versed in the subject, to consult with him on the best means of procedure. He said, "I'll only have four of you, as too many cooks spoil the broth." I took with me the late Mr. Odams of Bishops Stortford, who had done more to bring public opinion to bear on the question than any other man, and who had built a wharf on the banks of the Thames and fitted it up for "the slaughter of all foreign cattle on their debarkation," the principle for which we as a society had always contended. Mr. George Lepper, the eminent veterinary surgeon, was another; and I think Mr. John Treadwell was the fourth. The late Sir Philip Rose was with Mr. Disraeli, and after luncheon we adjourned to the library and went into the whole subject. Disraeli said he felt entirely with us as to our view that the only way to get rid of these diseases was to stamp them out by slaughter at the port of debarkation, but Ministers had to consider the opinions of the dwellers in the big towns of the North, who believed it would stop our foreign supply and tend to make meat dearer. We combated this opinion, and expressed our belief that it would have the contrary effect. Mr. Odams pointed out that the whole foreign supply of imported live meat only averaged $7\frac{1}{2}$ per cent., and asked if it were fair to jeopardize the $92\frac{1}{2}$ per cent. of our home cattle to keep up the importation of so insignificant an amount. This statement made a great impression upon Mr. Disraeli, and he immediately referred to the Board of Trade returns, and finding it was perfectly correct, promised to give us every support. I think he was at that time Chancellor of the Exchequer.

We all remarked on the perfectly business-like manner and the complete mastery of every detail he evinced whilst we were discussing the matter with him; and this

I have always heard was a characteristic of him—whenever he received a deputation he was "at home" in everything, and no one who had once had occasion to meet him dared to make any incorrect statement, as he would be down on him in a moment, fetch out his authority, and overwhelm him by either facts or figures.

I believe you obtain from many a public man in private conversation oftentimes a clearer insight into his opinions than you do by his public speeches. On one occasion I remarked to Disraeli that for several Sessions of Parliament I had never heard him even mention the word "Protection." He replied, "You may as well attempt to put life into the dead bones of a skeleton as to revive Protection in this country."

I think in one of his novels he says "that somehow or other if you meet the English country gentleman on the heated plains of India, on the deserts of Egypt, or on the icy slopes of the Alps, he has always a snug corner in his conversation to talk of Quarter Sessions." At our own Quarter Sessions dinners I have often heard him in conversation, and although not a great talker at the table, his remarks were so amusing and his sarcasm was so refined, that though severe, he was never ill-natured. I remember on one occasion the conversation turned on the newly-discovered fact that there were two dormant peerages in the Lowndes family—one in the Selby Lowndes of Whaddon, and another in the other county family of the same name, William Lowndes of Chesham, who owned a considerable property situated in Belgravia, comprising Lowndes Square and Chesham Place. Mr. Disraeli remarked that "somehow or other, if Cubitt (the great builder) built mansions and palaces over several acres of ground in the West End of London, a dormant peerage was almost sure to be found in the family of the owner."

When walking with him round Hughenden one day I remarked how interesting the whole district was, as being full of historic lore, and expressed my admiration of his residence. "Yes," he said, "it is interesting. The De Montforts lie in the church, and I have every reason to believe that Simon de Montfort resided here and left this house to compel King John to sign the Magna Charta." Ankerwyke is not more than twelve miles from Hughenden on the Buckinghamshire side of the Thames, while Magna Charta Island is in the middle of the river. King John came from Windsor on the Berks side, whilst the great Baron and his retainers were on the Bucks side, and the two parties met on this island as neutral ground. On another occasion at Hughenden I noticed to him how luxuriantly the trees grew, especially the cedars and the pines, and instanced a young cedar of Lebanon which had grown to a large size. He told me he had brought it himself with a few others from the valley of Lebanon when some years ago he travelled in Palestine, and that he had given one to Lady Grenville of Dropmore, a place about six miles distant, and that there was great rivalry between them as to which grew the best, her ladyship annually coming over to see his tree and compare notes, whilst he returned the visit. "I was always pleased," he said, "to find mine was far the finest specimen, notwithstanding old Frost, her gardener, took especial care of hers."

Mr. Disraeli purchased the Hughenden property about 1845, chiefly, I believe, to satisfy the country gentlemen that he was a landed proprietor like themselves, and that they should not throw in his teeth—which they to their shame had often done—that he was only an interloper and adventurer. Mr. Norris was the owner of the property, whose name in connection with his starting for the borough of Wycombe I have previously noticed. The price paid was, I think, £35,000, including the mansion and timber. Through his writings and Mrs. Disraeli's economic household management, he managed to raise £15,000, and borrowed £20,000 on mortgage, and, with care and frugality, managed to keep up the mansion and entertain his friends, greatly aided by his better half. I have heard some amusing stories of her excessive frugality. The following was told me by one who had ample means of knowing the circumstances. Mrs. Disraeli and her husband had come down from London to spend the Easter vacation at Hughenden, and had called on the various tradesmen at Wycombe to order the groceries and other requirements for their ten days' or fortnight's stay. It so happened that their sojourn was rather abruptly shortened, and Mrs. Disraeli was seen calling at the grocers and other purveyors, taking out of the carriage the non-consumed wares, and asking the shopkeepers to receive them back and have them re-weighed, and so to make a reduction in their accounts. The great statesman, with folded arms, was leaning back in the carriage looking perfectly nonchalant, but evidently desirous to have no share in the frugal transaction. I have heard many other stories of Mrs. Disraeli's peculiarities, and her parsimony was often carried to a ridiculous extent; however, it had the effect of ridding her husband of pecuniary troubles, and added to the great respect and affection he always entertained towards her, and which she amply deserved.

I am tempted to refer to the romance that proved so important a feature in Lord Beaconsfield's remarkable career. After the publication of each novel he was in the habit of receiving many congratulations from friends and literary people on the success of his works, and amongst others there came one from a lady of whom he knew nothing whatever, who lived in the neighbourhood of Torquay. She was in the habit of writing most enthusiastic praises, almost fulsome adulation, of his great abilities, not only as a writer but as a politician. He took but little notice of her except by formal letters of thanks, and thought no more of the matter. Some time afterwards, circumstances happened that took him and Mrs. Disraeli to the West of England, and they went to Torquay; then the thought struck him that he should find out who this Platonic lover could be, and in due course he discovered that she was a Miss Williams, a lady of some property, living in that neighbourhood. He determined to call and pay his respects to her. He did so, and the old lady was so thoroughly delighted that she could scarcely contain herself. At last she had obtained the object of her ambition, and had seen the great man for whom she had for years felt the deepest admiration. Mr. Disraeli prolonged his visit, and again called on her, and on his return to London forwarded her a set of his works, and continued to do so when any new publication of his appeared. Some few years afterwards this lady died, and, to his utter astonishment, left him all her fortune. This amounted to over £40,000, and it enabled him to pay off the whole of the encumbrances on his estate. This great benefactress was buried at Hughenden, and lies in the same vault containing the remains of the famous author and statesman and those of his wife.

I shall not soon forget the time when he first entered office, and, to the astonishment of every one, became Chancellor of the Exchequer. On the morning it was announced in *The Times* that he had accepted office, I was riding to the meet of the Staghounds, and Baron Lionel de Rothschild, father of the present Lord Rothschild, overtook me, and whilst riding onwards began talking of the new Derby Administration. I expressed my surprise at Mr. Disraeli being appointed to preside over the finances of the country, and doubted his capability for the office. The Baron replied, " The public make a great mistake. I know him well—his genius is equal to anything ; he will make a good Chancellor of the Exchequer, far better than Sir Charles Wood, Spring-Rice, and many others who have gone before him." This, coming from so eminent an authority as Baron Lionel, quite satisfied me, and I soon afterwards had occasion to find out that his opinion was justified.

A great agitation had commenced against a most obnoxious tax, " the post-horse duty," which was levied in a very objectionable manner, and was the last of the taxes which were "farmed," as it was called, or "let" to private individuals who exacted from the postmasters the uttermost farthing; and owing to the great uncertainty of the law, the grossest injustice in the shape of fines was perpetrated. I was one of a committee composed of members drawn from all parts of England to meet in London in order to press the Government for the removal or at least amelioration of this imposition. The then Chancellor of the Exchequer, Sir Charles Wood, afterwards Lord Halifax, received our deputation, and gave us so little encouragement to proceed that we came away in utter disgust, not only at the flippancy and absolute discourtesy to which we were subjected, but also with the crass ignorance he displayed in everything which related to the incidence of the tax. Soon after this disappointment of our hopes, Mr. Disraeli came into office; the same committee came together again to interview the new Chancellor, and one and all were filled with admiration at the tact, ability, and knowledge he showed on the occasion. We found him in his office in Downing Street ready to receive our deputation. Books and statistics were all prepared, the late Mr. Priestly, chief commissioner of stamps and taxes, stood at his elbow; with this gentleman Mr. Disraeli constantly consulted, and at each statement referred to the Blue Books before him, occasionally correcting the speakers if any inaccurate statements were put forward. In the end he promised us a full and favourable consideration of our complaints; unfortunately for us, he was out of office in a few months, and we had no opportunity of rectifying our grievances.

Not long after Disraeli's memorable visit to Manchester on April 3rd, 1872, I had an opportunity of speaking to him of his reception there, and he said he thought he had never been so heartily received anywhere as in that city. I mentioned that I had intimate friends resident at Manchester, and that I heard from them that no public man, not even Mr. John Bright, had received such a welcome. I proceeded to mention several salient points of his address, which, I remarked, bore out many of the opinions which had been fully expressed by him in his earlier novels, especially upon the franchise, to all which he still seemed thoroughly to adhere. Even now I recall a few memorable sentences of this speech in the Free Trade Hall. In speaking of the Reform Act, he said, "Lord Grey in his measure of 1832, which was, no doubt, on the whole a statesmanlike measure, committed a great, and, for the time, it appeared an irretrievable error. By that measure he not only made no provision for the representation of the working-classes in the Constitution, but he absolutely abolished those ancient franchises which the working-classes had enjoyed and exercised from time immemorial. That was the origin of Chartism, and of that electoral uneasiness which existed in this country more or less for thirty years." He said to me that "he was sure I must have remembered that he had on several occasions in our County Hall said that the Reform Bill of 1832 was a disfranchising measure," and I alluded to the disfranchisement of the ancient Potwaller and the old Freemen. In reference to education he spoke with his usual strong yet cautious manner: "The public mind will arrive at conclusions which you may call Dogmas and Formularies and prescribe by Acts of Parliament; but I am persuaded that a system of national education which repudiates the religious instincts of our nature will be the greatest of failures, but more fatal to the State than to the Church." How truly also he hit the right nail on the head, when he said, in this Manchester speech of h's, " Gentlemen, *political institutions are the embodied experience of a race.*"

Disraeli was always particularly anxious for the welfare of the agricultural labourer, and I do not forget how, in one of his speeches at the meeting of the Bucks Agricultural Association, in speaking of the sanitary condition and the better housing of the labourers, he said, " In building cottages there are three absolutely necessary things to be provided—an oven, a tank, and a porch." This is practical advice; and in his Manchester speech I find the following, which perhaps may shock the sensitive nerves of many of my agricultural friends. " And in the first place," he said, " to prevent any misconception, I beg to express my opinion that an agricultural labourer has as much right to combine for the bettering of his condition as a manufacturing labourer or a worker in metals." Again, he said, " Gentlemen, I should deeply regret to see the tillage of this country reduced and a recurrence to pasture take place. I should regret it principally on account of the labourers themselves. Their new friends call them 'Hodge,' and describe them as a feeble body, and stolid in mind. That is not my experience of them —I believe them to be a stalwart race, sufficiently shrewd and open to reason. I would say to them with confidence, as the great Athenian said to the Spartan who rudely assailed him, 'Strike, but hear me.'" A capital instance of the rich humour in which his speeches abound!

Illustrating how the public generally are mistaken in estimating the earnings of the agricultural labourer, I told him I had every year taken out from my labour-book the annual earnings of my *ordinary* workmen—not my carters, shepherds, cowmen, or Sunday men as we call them—and found they averaged 17s. 9d. per week, and that the larger their families, after a certain age, the better off they were; that I had several men who had one or two boys, under fourteen years of age, working on the farms, who supplemented the standing wages of their father of 14s. per week by at least 4s. to 5s. each, this bringing up their weekly wage to 23s. to 25s. per week; and as they had for each family a really good cottage and large garden for 1s. 6d. per week, they were practically better off than men in the manufacturing districts, where wages averaged from 28s. to 30s. per week, with high rents for inferior dwellings. Lord Beaconsfield replied, "That from his personal knowledge, not only of Hughenden, but other districts of the country, he had no hesitation in saying that the improvement in the lot of the rural labourer during the past fifty years was most remarkable, and that their toil, by the introduction of improved machinery, and also by the introduction of the allotment system, was not so severe as of old." This I endorsed, and said we could scarcely get any one, except old men, to use the flail for thrashing, and only a few who even knew how to handle and sharpen the scythe. But I might cover pages with notes of Disraeli's comments on matters with which I myself was intimately acquainted ; his conversations convinced me that Lord Beaconsfield had mastered the politics of country life, and was ready with remedies which he felt would be of use.

I cannot refrain from quoting one more extract from Mr. Disraeli's Manchester speech, so exactly applicable is it to the present time. Speaking on the licensing question, he said, "I doubt not there is in this hall more than one publican who remembers that last year an Act was introduced to declare that all publicans were sinners. I doubt not there are in this hall widows and orphans who remember the profligate proposition to plunder their lonely heritage." And that masterpiece of illustration, "The unnatural stimulus of the Ministry was subsiding. Their paroxysms ended in prostration. As I sit opposite the Treasury Bench the Ministers remind me of one of those marine landscapes not unusual on the coast of South America. You behold a range of exhausted volcanoes. Not a flame flickers on a single pallid crest, but the situation is still dangerous. There are occasional earthquakes, and ever and anon the dark rumbling of the sea."

These reminiscences of Lord Beaconsfield merely record what may seem commonplace anecdotes and remarks; others will present to the world the higher attributes of his statesmanship, but my hope is that probably some of the anecdotes, which people may call trivialities, tend to show the inner mind and life of a great man when untrammelled by weighty problems of State. At the funeral of this great statesman I was privileged to enter the church. Never shall I forget the solemn scene, for never before in history was anything like it. The procession was honoured by the presence of the Prince of Wales and his royal brothers, foreign ambassadors, most of the leading inhabitants of the county, by even those who had been his greatest opponents, men like Lord Hartington and Sir William Harcourt. One alone was conspicuous by his absence. He had *missed his train at Paddington!* The beauty of the surrounding neighbourhood, of the village church and churchyard standing in the park at Hughenden, the truly sylvan landscape, the quiet of the "beech-clad Chilterns," the crowds of sobbing, reverential villagers, the respectful grief of his tenantry, formed a picture never to be forgotten, while this last tribute of respect, to one of the most remarkable men of this or any other age or country, was being paid. No one more deeply mourned his loss than the writer of these memories. The monument erected to the memory of his father, Isaac Disraeli, by his devoted wife, over-topping the park at Hughenden, and the restoration of the beautiful parish church itself, will of themselves perpetuate the name and reputation of Benjamin Disraeli, Earl of Beaconsfield, K.G., whose dust now mingles with ancient champions of the people's rights, in the church containing the ashes of those noble crusaders, the De Montforts, names ever to be associated with the most stirring events in the history of England's freedom.

CHAPTER V.

Bordeaux and Epernay in 1868—An Incident at Chambord—
Messrs. Nathaniel Johnstone: their Vineyards at Dausac—The
Manufacture of Claret—Mr. Moët's Vineyards at Epernay—
The Manufacture of Champagne—National Tastes in Wine
—Longevity—" Ways and Means " Lowndes.

HAVING some spare time at my disposal after harvest in the year 1868, I determined to pay a long-contemplated visit to the wine districts of France, especially the claret and champagne countries, and in the second week of September started with two young friends on a tour of inspection. Our travels were more prolonged than we had intended, as the vintage was not yet in full swing; but I shall not weary my readers with any description of them. At Chambord, I remember, after lingering some time in the splendid château, we proceeded to a small hotel in its neighbourhood, and, ordering a bottle of champagne and some light repast, we went into a room, where two well-dressed countrymen were seated. The smart, pretty-looking girl who brought in our wine, pointed to a moderately-executed engraving hanging on the wall, and said, " Messieurs, voilà le Comte de Chambord." I said, " Oui, le roi de France—Henri V." The two men, jumping up, embraced me enthusiastically—the girl was equally excited; they scarcely knew how to express themselves, so delighted were they that we dared to speak out boldly. It showed at once how truly the old Royalist feeling still existed in this valley of the Loire.

At Macau, a place on the banks of that not very attractive stream, the Garonne, Mr. Arthur Johnstone met us with his carriage and horses to take us to his château at Dausac. Here we were received most kindly by the mother of our host and his father, Mr. Nathaniel Johnstone, the head of the great firm. With them we visited their vineyards to see the gathering of the grapes, and the whole process of making the celebrated "Claret," a title which, of course, is almost unknown in France, as all the wine of that district is called "Vin de Bordeaux," and then named after the estate or property, as "Lafitte," "Margaux," and so on.

The grapes, gathered carefully in baskets, are carried to waggons in which rest two large wicker panniers. Each waggon is drawn by two bullocks, of a light brown or dun colour, with wide-spreading horns of large size. These carts are drawn up to an opening in the wall of the factory; the grapes are thrown on to an inclined plane, whence the bunches slide down on to a sieve or wire table, by which stand fine-looking, cleanly men, with bared arms, who pick out the unripe or decayed grapes and scratch or rub them through this coarse sieve. The grapes and juice fall through into a trough underneath, the bunch and stalks being left behind, and the grapes, some of which are crushed and others whole, are then carried in large vessels and poured into mighty vats, holding many hundreds of gallons, where the wine begins to ferment in a few hours—about eight or ten; those grapes which have not been crushed burst of themselves, the juice falls to the bottom, and the skins and seed-pips and pieces of stalk float on the top. The vat is continually filled up till it will hold no more. The mass of skins and stalks soon becomes solid and forms a sort of handcake of considerable thickness on the top, and thus partly preserves the wine. The fermentation is allowed to go on unchecked, but is carefully watched until the spring, when all fermentation is exhausted. The wine is then drawn off from the bottom of the vat and put into smaller vessels, conveniently placed for closer examination. Whilst fermenting the casks are continually filled up, until about a year is passed, when they are racked off and are left for another year.

The liquor is then fit for shipment, but the higher class wines are kept for another year, and the *premiers crus*, of which there are only four, namely, "Lafitte," "Latour," "Châteaux Margaux," and "Haut Brion," generally for four years before their final bottling. Amongst the *seconds crus* are "Mouton Rothschild," "La Rose," "Cos Destournel," "Léoville," "Châteaux Palmer," and many others; and in the *troisièmes crus* are "La Grange," "Ducru Baucailleux"; *quatrièmes crus*, "St. Julien," "St. Estephe," "Mouton D'Armaillac"; while in the *cinquièmes crus*, or fifth growth, "Pontet Canet" heads the list, with at least twelve or fifteen more; and all below these are unclassed wines, many however of excellent quality in certain seasons.

Old Mr. Johnstone told me that they have annually a

grand dinner of the *Syndicate of Bordeaux*, which is considered one of the most important and finest dinners of the kind in France. A special wine is provided with each course, to gradually educate the palate until the acme of perfection in taste is attained. At their last dinner, the wine for which the highest position had been assigned was "Pontet Canet" of 1858, which in that year, although a fifth growth, took precedence of "Lafitte" and all other wines. The seasons have a marked effect on some estates; in the year 1867 the "Châteaux Margaux" was sold at 9*d.* per bottle! We were shown the "Caves" of this noted Johnstone firm, in which were stored over 20,000 hhds. of claret, and over 1,000,000 bottles, many of them of the choicest vintages. I had always been a considerable purchaser of claret, and Mr. Harry Johnstone showed me the wines of 1865 reserved for me, which I had bought in the year 1867, and I think I never drank anything better flavoured. They were "Lafitte," "Latour," "Mouton Rothschild," "Cos Destournel," and "La Rose." They were in the highest condition, and were sent over to me for bottling in the spring of 1869, and I, who ought not to, may say that they exceptionally did honour to their selection. I have some of the first-named still left, and certainly it is a grand wine.

I remember that the general election for the Chamber of Deputies was going on whilst we were in Bordeaux, and Mr. Nathaniel Johnstone, junr., was a candidate for the district. He was an Imperialist, and the house of which he was a member took the greatest interest in his success. He was fortunate in getting elected by a considerable majority. His election was petitioned against on the ground that he was an alien; he however proved his nationality, as his father and himself had become naturalized some years before.

After this most enjoyable visit we returned to Paris, where I was glad to meet my two eldest daughters at the Hôtel du Louvre, where they had arrived on the same day from Boulogne. I left my two young travelling companions to escort them around Paris, whilst I went on a visit to my friends, Messrs. Moët and Chandon, the chiefs of the noted Epernay House, celebrated throughout the world for their well-known brands of champagne. I was fortunate, after a delightful journey from Paris, in finding the head of the firm at home —a fine old gentleman of courtly and most agreeable manners, who treated me in the kindest way, and walked with me through the town of Epernay up to the hills to his extensive vineyards, by far the largest in France. The vintage had begun, so that I was in time to see the gathering of the grapes by hundreds of men, women, and children, assembled together from all quarters—a most picturesque scene. After walking a long time the old gentleman—then of seventy-seven years of age, walking briskly by my side—looking over the valley of the Marne, which river formed a beautiful addition to the landscape, pointed out the various districts visible from the high ground on which we stood. Aÿ about five miles away, Sillery a little below us, Bouzy almost adjoining; but the chief district was Epernay itself, where Messrs. Moët have 1200 acres of vineyards.

I was surprised to find that they grew chiefly a black grape, the vine being trained close to the ground, and looking very different to the vineyards of Bordeaux, where the vines are carefully trained upwards of seven feet high, the bunches reminding you of an English hot-house; but at Epernay the bunches are small and hard, and are like the grapes grown on the walls of cottages in our country. The grapes from which the " white dry Sillery " is made are white, but the juice is blended with a small portion of the black grape.

We next visited the buildings where the wine was made, an operation quite different from that employed at Bordeaux. Here the grapes, being put into a press, the juice is squeezed out, the skins remaining behind, and as the colouring matter is derived from the skin, the wine is of a slight pink colour, in many instances only a pale amber. It would need too long a description to give *seriatim* the various processes the wine undergoes before it reaches the consumer. With the best classes of champagne it takes three years before it is fit for consumption; the manipulating and disgorging in the second year, the corking, wiring, stringing, tinfoiling, or waxing—all this costing infinite care and labour, and this is in addition to that most essential operation, the preparation and mixing of the liqueur. Whatever may be said of " Brut " wine, I believe every bottle made has a certain amount of liqueur in it, even as low as 1 per cent.; the generality has about 3 per cent., and the richer wines, still preferred by some people, have 5 per cent., whilst the wines consumed by the French people themselves and the Germans have

7 per cent., and the Austrians and Russians, who chiefly consume "Madame Clicquots" and "Roederers," have even more.

The Americans, liking their champagne rather sweet, prefer Piper's wines. The chief firms who ship to England, and whose wines are in the highest repute, are Perrier Jouet, Pommery, Heidseck, Ernest Irroy, Giesler, Lanson, Ayala, Jules Mumm, and Pol Roger; but Moët's has by far the largest consumption in England, and their "Brut Impérial" is equal to any of the most noted shippers. Many manufacturers of champagne are not growers; they are purchasers of the wine of the farmers in the various districts, manipulating them according to the tastes of their customers. Messrs. Simon and Kingscote, the representatives of Messrs. Moët and Chandon in England, import enormous quantities, almost reaching a million bottles per annum. *A propos* of sweet and dry wine, I cannot forbear giving old Mr. Moët's opinion on the subject. I remarked "that the English people thought the champagne shipped to this country was too sweet, and that we should like it as they drink it in France." "Ah!" said he, "that is a great mistake; you English are the driest people in the world. The Russians are the sweetest, next to them Prussians, then the French and Belgians, then the Americans, and you English the driest."

With regard to the addition of the liqueur, he said, "What do you do with your strawberries? You add a little sugar, it brings out the flavour of the strawberry; you take the melon on your plate, you shake a little sugar over it, and it brings out the flavour of the melon;

that is all we do to our wine. We know from a century of study what our wines want, and we can prepare them accordingly. If you want 'Brut' wine you can have it, but all champagnes want a little something to bring out the highest flavour of the grapes." And this opinion, from a long experience of the taste of many eminent judges of wine in England, I can strongly endorse. I remember I also remarked jokingly whilst on the hill-sides in the midst of his vineyards, that I did not see any gooseberry-trees or rhubarb. He answered seriously but good-humouredly, and said, "That is another folly of your people and shows their ignorance. We can get more juice out of an acre of vines than out of three or four acres devoted to the cultivation of either of the vegetables you mention, and I believe you would not find as many rhubarb plants in the many miles of country you are overlooking as you find in half an acre of any gardens round London."

I little thought when I was visiting this fair land and marvelling at its beauty and fruitfulness, and seeing in every direction the result of centuries of thought, labour, and skill, that in less than two years it was to be over-run and occupied by thousands of foreign troops on their hostile march to Paris; yet with all the German hatred of the French, and the memory of the years of misery and degradation that they underwent, under a greater Napoleon than the then ruler of France, Napoleon III., the German troops carefully protected the people of this district, and I was told that a record was kept of every bottle of wine the soldiers consumed, and that it was all honestly paid for. My kind old friend, Mr.

Moët, left his home at this time, and went to Jersey, where he resided until the German occupation terminated, when he returned to his ancestral home and died at the patriarchal age of eighty-two years.

I think to live to such a ripe age, as did Mr. Moët, is less rare now than it used to be. Sir George Cornewall Lewis asserted that there are no thoroughly authenticated cases of centenarians; but that there are cases of undoubted certainty I am convinced, and for one of them I can personally vouch. An old lady, a Mrs. Grace, died in the year 1877, who was certainly born in 1776; she had been a Miss Rickford before her marriage, sister to William Rickford, the banker, and Member of Parliament for the Borough. Born in the town, baptized there, married there, she lived all her life at Aylesbury, and there can be no doubt but that she was the identical lady whose birth and baptism in 1776 appeared in the parish registry. Had she been a daughter of some poor person, such errors as Sir George Lewis indicated might have been possible, but she was known to every one, a lady moving always in a good position. On Mrs. Grace attaining her hundredth year, I took her a bouquet of choice flowers, culled from my greenhouse, and found her perfectly sensible and cheerful; only her eyesight had failed her.

I can myself well remember seeing the Hon. T. Grenville, great-uncle to the late Duke of Buckingham, passing through Aylesbury in the year 1835, on a visit to Stowe: he was fond of relating that when a boy at Eton, he and some companions used to congregate round an old man to hear him tell stories which his grandfather, who had stood as one of the sentinels at the execution of Charles I., had told him! I myself therefore have seen a man who wanted only one link to connect him with the reign of Charles I., a period of over two hundred and forty years! To instance another case. In the year 1837 my father became tenant of Broughton Farm, which then belonged to Mr. Richard Lowndes, who had been at one time a barrister on circuit, and from his manner of cross-examining witnesses, nicknamed "Bother 'em Lowndes." This old gentleman granted my father a lease of the farm for fourteen years, and after signing it, said, "Now, Mr. Fowler, I am only granting you this lease for your own protection, for I am beyond the age of a man" (he was over eighty years of age), "and I hope you will enjoy the tenancy after I am gone." He lived to grant my father another lease for fourteen years. I recollect old Mr. Lowndes taking a great-nephew of his upon his knee, and saying to him, "I have many a time had your father on my knee, and your grandfather and I were brothers. Ah!" he continued, "and I can remember well my grandfather, and he was Chancellor of the Exchequer to Queen Anne!" To this Chancellor of the Exchequer is attributed one of the most popular axioms in the English language. He was looking over the shoulders of one of the junior clerks in the Treasury, and saw by his casting up of some accounts that he was wrong. "Oh," said the clerk, "it is only a few pence!" "Never you mind that," said the astute Chancellor; "you take care of the pence, the pounds will take care of themselves."

CHAPTER VI.

Steeplechasing in the year 1835—The Great Race at Aylesbury: Captain Beecher wins from Mr. Allnutt—The Races the year following: Jem Mason is too clever—The Royal Hunt Club: Anecdotes of a Horse in their Dining-Room—Anecdotes of the Rev. C. Erle and Bishop Wilberforce—Mr. Carroll's Horses, Family, and Jokes.

THE annals of the steeplechase proper seem to commence in the year 1834, when the first important event of acknowledged record came off at St. Albans, where the renowned horses, Moonraker and Grimaldi, made so great a sensation. St. Albans can boast of having provided the course for the first great public steeplechase, but I have always held that Aylesbury had the right to second honours.

One evening, at the celebrated "Crockfords" Club, discussing the peculiarities of the various hunting districts in England, Mr. Henry Peyton, the eldest son of that "prince of whips," Sir Henry Peyton—whose yellow drag and faultless team of greys with their brightly kept brass harness, with "Old George," his esteemed stud-groom, and Joe Buswell his second man "perched up aloft" behind him, were a thing of renown in the "Good Old Times"—spoke of the difficulties of crossing the Vale of Aylesbury, mentioning especially the brooks which intersected the course afterwards selected. This was questioned by some of the noble sportsmen present, and the conversation ended by a promise from Mr. Peyton that he would undertake to give them a fair four-mile course over a hunting country which he himself had often ridden, and which he stated that men hunting in that district were compelled to face if they rode fairly to hounds like sportsmen. It should be noted that at that time Mr. Peyton was allowed to be one of the best cross-country riders in England. His proposal was accepted, and he determined to carry it out. He consulted his friend, Captain Lamb, on the subject, and the latter undertook to find a silver cup of fifty guineas as a prize, and the following conditions were drawn up and agreed to—Each horse to carry 12st. 7lbs., twenty guineas entrance P.P., the second horse to save his stake; and the race was fixed to come off within one month. When the entries were closed, it was found that there were twenty-one horses entered.

On the night before the race the head-quarters of the committee, the White Hart at Aylesbury, was crowded with the *élite* of the sporting world; every inn was filled, and stables were at a premium. There was no railway then to the town, and as the race was timed for twelve o'clock, there was but little chance of visitors from London arriving in time unless they came overnight. The course determined on was from Waddesdon wind-mill, about four and a half miles from Aylesbury, to a field in front of the church, the steeple of which forms a distinctive feature in the district and for some miles round. There is a small grass enclosure in front of the wind-mill, and the whole line, excepting about three acres of allotment and gardens near the town, was then under grass. The fences were left in their natural state, untrimmed, and were not only formidable in aspect, but really difficult to negotiate. The course was most severe, and comprised several doubles and tall bullfinchers, ox fences with post and rails, big singles, one cross road, one deeply-rutted lane, one fairly-sized brook, one thick spinney, and the river Thame, about twenty-eight feet wide! This line ran parallel with the turnpike road, so that a horseman riding along it was able to keep abreast of the runners, and could see nearly every fence jumped. No flags marked the course, and until the morning of the race the line of country was kept a profound secret, for fear that any of the proposed riders should avail himself of the opportunity of seeing the fences and thus find out any weak place in the obstacles to be encountered.

On the morning of the race the company thronged the whole line of the turnpike road. The course to be taken was announced for the first time, but no flags whatever were used except the usual two in the winning field. The horses, with their riders mounted, left the White Hart and other inns, after weighing in the yard of the head-quarters. The colours worn by the riders were of unusual brilliance, and my memory enables me to recollect a trivial incident, which I remember telling to the late Lady Brassey, celebrated for her *Voyage in the Sunbeam*. Whilst weighing, Mr. Allnutt, Lady Brassey's father, appeared in a very resplendent satin jacket of purple and green plaid, and Mr. Peyton stroked it and said, " How pretty. I wonder if it will be as clean as now at the end of the race." Lady Brassey told me that she had that very jacket at home, and that her father had always treasured it as a memorable record of that great race.

At the time I speak of I was a boy who had just left school, and as every horse in the town was engaged, I was glad to get a mount on an old grey post-horse with a post-boy's saddle with a crupper, and, thus equipped, I stationed myself close to the Stone Bridge river, where I lingered for some time regarding the strange and novel scene. Twenty horses with their riders faced the starter, who thus addressed the competitors: " Do you see Aylesbury church-steeple ? "—" Yes."—" Well, when you get near it, you will see two red flags in a field ; now the first horse that passes between those two flags will win the race ; none of you must go on to the turnpike road or you will be disqualified. Are you ready ? "— " Yes."—Then " Off" ; and away they sped on their perilous journey. *Bell's Life* describes the race, but my personal recollection is that at the river twelve or more seemed to be racing at it together, and I counted, a moment after, thirteen floating about and struggling to get out in a disorderly crowd. The Marquis of Waterford, who rode his nearly-thoroughbred horse Lancet, put him at the river at a splitting pace, but as soon as his fore-feet touched the bank he fell backwards. The poor horse was got out with great difficulty after being in the water a long time, and a fortnight after died in the White Hart stable at Aylesbury from the injuries received while being pulled out of the river. Mr. Allnutt, on the grey mare Laurestina, was the first out of the river, and sailed gallantly away at least a long field ahead, before ever old Martin Beecher, on a well-known rat-tailed horse, Vivian, could get well on his way. He had ridden his horse gently down the bank into the water, and once on the other side flung himself off on to the land, and pulled his horse out, remounted, and set off in hot pursuit of the mare. That veteran sportsman, John Brown of Tring, still living, though about ninety years of age—immortalized by the poetical description of the "Bag Fox," when Lord Lonsdale hunted with his well-known harriers—was on his famous hunter, Confidence, and had a regular souser: no novelty however to him, as he always fearlessly rode to hounds at everything which came in his way. Then the young jockey, Jem Mason, one of the finest and most accomplished horsemen who ever appeared in the pigskin, made his *début* in public on Mr. Tilbury's Prospero. Mr. Anderson, I think, rode his own horse, The Poet. But each and every one found the bottom of the river, and many of them did not make any attempt afterwards to overtake the leading horses.

In the end, Laurestina, after keeping the lead for the whole distance from the river, fell from sheer distress into the winning field, and old Beecher, on Vivian, slipped past her and won cleverly. Mr. Allnutt quickly remounted and came in second, whilst the third place was awarded to Prospero. Captain Lamb, the owner of Vivian, won only a small stake, as plunging on steeplechases was but little practised in those days.

This race was the prelude to many more in the Aylesbury Vale, and in the year 1836 two of the most celebrated steeplechases of the day were run during the February meeting of the Royal Hunt. The first was a heavy-weight race, for horses carrying 12st. 7lbs., and was run early in the day, on Tuesday, so that the hounds could meet after the conclusion of the race. Vivian, again steered by Beecher, was the favourite, but was beaten a short length by Saladin, ridden by Powell; perhaps the Captain had made too sure. This race was marked by many mishaps, one of which was the crippling for life of Billy Bean, who after scuttling through a deep brook came to a stiff bullfincher, and, in steering his horse through a gap near a tree, caught his leg against the trunk, and broke his knee-cap.

On the Thursday the light-weight race was run, each horse carrying 11st. 7lbs., and many of the same horses competed as on Tuesday. Here the rat-tailed veteran, Vivian, won an exciting race; Grimaldi, the old grey of St. Albans notoriety, being second; The Pony, third; and, I think, the winner's former competitor, Laurestina, was fourth. It was a splendid race over one of the stiffest countries in England. The start was at Waddesdon, and the course was on the opposite side of the road to that of 1835. The finish was at Quarrendon. The Marquis of Waterford fell two fences from home, and his horse, Yellow Dwarf, was very much injured. He rode himself, and felt sure of winning, but came to grief at a great double which he attempted to clear at one stride. Jem Mason was first favourite. He rode a splendid horse, of great power and much speed. In the middle of the race was a very stiff fence, and in it was an old gateway, railed up with very strong rails, which it was supposed no horse would attempt to jump. The night before the race the two upper rails were sawn nearly in two, so as just to hang together. This had been done privately, and Jem was told to ride full swing at it, and once safely over, he would have a great advantage over the rest of the field; but the "little game" was discovered, and early in the morning an extra rail, doubly strong, was inserted, and the unsuspicious Jem rode confidently at this obstacle. The horse struck the rail, came over a tremendous cropper, and lost all chance of the race.

The fame of the Aylesbury Vale country, both as a hunting and steeplechasing centre, became now firmly established. The races usually took place about eleven o'clock, and the turn-out of the stag about half-past twelve, and after a jovial club dinner in the evening, the company were generally well tired out; but still it left time for many a joke and a freak. On one occasion the Marquis of Waterford brought his horse up-stairs into the dining-room. Lord Jocelyn and Mr. Ricardo led the horse up the garden steps, which were very steep indeed, took him into the dining-room and round the table, gave him some apples and biscuits, which he ate, and then commenced to get him down-stairs. It was useless to attempt his descent by the same stairs, so steep were they, so he was led round the corridor to the front staircase, which was easy of descent. The floor of the passage was polished oak, and, although carpeted in the middle, the horse slipped badly, and at the head of the stairs obstinately refused to move one jot. At last he began kicking, smashed the passage windows, and soon cleared a ring behind him; Lord Jocelyn and his comrade resolutely sticking to his head. Eventually when a little quieted they blindfolded him, and, once he began to descend, he could not stop, and blundered down into the entrance hall, having done himself no injury; and, excepting to a few banisters and the smashing of some windows, but little damage was done. This was the first attempt which had been made of bringing a horse up-stairs as a visitor, and must not be confounded with the far more remarkable feat which I shall describe hereafter, performed some years afterwards in the same room.

Most of these sporting celebrities have been gathered to their forefathers, but the staid and steady member for Warwickshire, Mr. Newdegate, scarcely seems yet to have left us, so fresh his memory; and that prince of companions, Mr. Lorraine Baldwin, will, I am sure, look back with pleasure, mingled with some regret, at the jolly days he passed with the Royal Hunt at the White Hart at Aylesbury.

Amongst the invited guests who were privileged to meet at the select dinner-table was the Rev. Christopher Erle, the esteemed though eccentric Rector of Hardwick, a small village about four miles from Aylesbury. He generally was seen at the meet of the Royal and Mr. de Burgh's Staghounds, and was a great favourite with all the Masters of the Buckhounds. Mr. Erle was brother of the late Lord Chief Justice Erle, and was a ripe classical scholar, well known, when a Fellow of New

College, Oxford, as a genial, kind-hearted man, and it was not till late in life that he was inducted into the tolerably rich college living of Hardwick. It was my privilege to enjoy his friendship, as amongst my most agreeable recollections. My own school training enabled me to appreciate his sayings and to enjoy the Latin and Greek puns and witticisms he was so fond of telling. One thing alone which he did when he was accustomed to dine with the Hunt Club was enough to declare his goodness of heart and kindness to the poor. The host was surprised to find Mr. Erle, the first time he came into Aylesbury, after he had been the guest of the Master of the Buckhounds, asking how much the dinner bill had come to? He was told it was of no consequence, as his dinner was charged to the Master of the Buckhounds. This did not satisfy him, and at last, on being told the amount, varying as it did from twenty-five to thirty shillings per head, we found that the next day he went round and distributed the amount amongst the old and deserving poor of his parish and the neighbouring hamlet of Weedon. His heart was always open to any tale of distress, and his pocket also.

Many stories are told of this reverend sportsman, some relating also to the late Bishop of Oxford, Dr. Wilberforce, who was very fond of Mr. Erle, and was always glad to get a "rise" out of his country rector. As the following anecdote has had many variations, I venture here to give the version related to me by Mr. Erle himself. Sir Thomas Digby Aubrey, who lived at Oving, a parish adjoining that of Mr. Erle, had invited the Bishop to dinner, and several of the neighbouring gentry and clergy to meet him, and amongst others the Reverend Christopher. Now, the reverend gentleman was very fond of going to see the hounds meet, and, pottering along through a well-known line of gates, generally managed to see a good deal of fun. The Bishop, hearing of this, thought it would be a good opportunity to trot Mr. Erle out at Sir Thomas's dinner-party, and in conversation said he had a great objection to his clergy riding to hounds, and, with a merry twinkle of his eye, alluded pointedly to the worthy Rector. Mr. Erle, in reply, said that he saw no harm in it, and that people who went to the carnal enjoyment of balls were equally reprehensible with men who occasionally went to a meet of the hounds; and he deemed it his duty, he said, to allude to a statement in the *Court Circular* of the past week, in which it mentioned that amongst the guests at Her Majesty's State Ball at Buckingham Palace was the Bishop of Oxford! A great laugh ensued, and his lordship replied, "Yes, Mr. Erle, but I make it a rule never to go into the room where the dancers are." The ready retort was, "Exactly my case, my lord; for I make it a rule never to be in the same field where the hounds are running." There was an explosion of laughter at this, at the Bishop's expense, in which his lordship heartily joined, when the Rector added he did not much care for hunting, and seldom went with any but Baron Rothschild's hounds, as he wished particularly "to promote Christianity amongst the Jews."

My good old friend came to tell me this story a few days afterwards with this amusing addition. The

Bishop had come into the neighbourhood to hold a series of confirmations in various parishes, and the day after the dinner-party he was to be at Quainton, about three miles from Hardwick. Mr. Erle was, as usual, *pottering* along after the Baron's hounds (a Miss Potter, a very smart horsewoman, being out, who much pleased him), when, feeling somewhat thirsty, and knowing that the Rector of Quainton's wife carried at her girdle a bunch of keys, one of which opened a tap of exceedingly good home-brewed beer, he hung his horse to the gate of the gardens leading up to the Rectory, dismounted, and boldly walked up the path leading to the front door. What was his dismay at meeting (as he described it) a grand funeral procession of clergy, headed by a pair of lawn sleeves—no other than his censor, the Bishop. "What do you think I did?" said he. "Sprang behind the laurels, and hid myself, like Adam and Eve in Paradise, *while* the Lord *passed by*." His horse had to be removed to allow his lordship to pass into the church which was adjoining, and none of them were aware of the identity of the owner. It need not be said that the worthy Rector trotted home to Hardwick, and there was no more *pottering* that day.

On one occasion when the hounds were running pretty hard, the Duke de Grammont, who was a tolerably good man across country, got into the Cublington brook. Baron Lionel de Rothschild was there, and did not attempt to jump it, but was very solicitous to get the Duke out of the water safely. Mr. Erle was there also, and strongly urged the Baron to go in and fetch the Duke out, which the Baron resolutely declined to do, notwithstanding all Mr. Erle's arguments and entreaties. Some time afterwards the Baron asked him why he was so anxious to get him into the brook? The Rector told him, if he had once got him in he would have kept him there "till he had baptized him and made him a Christian." The hounds met annually at Hardwick, which meant the Rectory, where a famous breakfast was laid out, to which all were bidden to attend. There was always a fine ham in the centre of the table, which he persistently would press Baron Meyer to partake of, as he could assure him it was a *mutton* ham. On one occasion Sir Robert Peel was at the meet there with Lady Peel and the Baroness, and many ladies from Mentmore. Soon after the start, Sir Robert had a fall. Mr. Erle assisted him to mount; in fact, as he told me the next day, he tried to *Mount Pelion Ossa*. Lady Peel lost a fur cloak at the same time, which was afterwards found, whereupon the Rector wrote a poem chiefly composed of Latin and Greek quotations, but saying that it had been at last found in *Houndsditch*, where doubtless it had been taken by some of the party. Baron Meyer was justly offended at this, and although he put up with many of Mr. Erle's eccentricities, he thought this was going too far, and for some long time afterwards he was excluded from the Mentmore parties, where he had up to that time always been a most welcome guest.

Poor dear old Rector! how much you were beloved, how truly charitable you were! I well remember once your accompanying your brother, the Lord Chief Justice, on a visit to my farm on horseback to see the mowing-machine which was then just new, and the first ever used in the Vale of Aylesbury, and how pleased the Chief Justice was. The machine did its work well, although one of the earliest ever turned out by Walter Wood. It had a wooden frame, and was made at Hoosick Falls, U.S., America, and Colonel Cranston (Mr. Wood's partner) came down specially to drive and start it. The Rev. Christopher Erle died at a ripe old age, and was buried in Hartwell Churchyard, regretted by all who knew him. By his will he left a considerable sum of money to build a convalescent ward to the Bucks General Infirmary.

Mr. Wm. Carroll, of Suffolk Street, Pall Mall, was wine merchant to the Royal Hunt Club, as he had been an original member of the club, but a little extra gaiety and sport had brought down "his noble to ninepence." Carroll was an Irishman of the most genial type, and as a post-prandial conversationalist he has been rarely equalled. Some of his stories would be a little too broad for publication nowadays, but one he told with great gusto, and with his richest of all rich brogues, I well remember. Before the Roman Catholic Relief Bill was passed, every Irish voter was asked before he polled, of what religion he was? Of course every scheme was tried to evade the question, for if he proved to be a Roman Catholic the vote was lost. Tim Raffety presented himself at the polling-booth at one of the Irish borough elections, and was asked the usual question, "What religion are ye?" Answer, "Bi gor, sor, and I am the same religion as me forefathers."— "Come, Tim, that won't do; tell us plainly." No other answer could be obtained. Then the clerk tried another, and said, "Of what persuasion are you?" "By jabers," said Tim, who gave a rollicking flourish with his shillelagh, "I should like to see the man a persuading o' me!" Several other plans were tried, and no satisfactory answer was given. At last, in despair, he was asked, "Of what way of thinking are you?"—"Well, sor, I am the same way of thinking as me landlady." —"Why, Tim, that's no answer; what does she think?" "Well, sor," answered Tim, "I owe her seven pound ten for rint, and she thinks I shall never pay her, and so do I."

Mr. Carroll gave my father a slight sketch of his life. He was the son of an Irish landed gentleman of fair fortune. "On coming into my property," he said, "I was soon one of the gayest of the gay. I went to London, joined in all the fast doings of the day, and, when the hunting season began, went to Melton with a stud of nine horses, and lived well up to my income and a little beyond it. In about two years I married, and sold a hunter, leaving me with eight; before the season came round I had a dear little daughter born—I sold a hunter; the next year the same thing occurred—I sold a hunter. I was left then with five horses, but I thought I could still get my five days a week; but before the next season I had another daughter—I sold a hunter. I then thought it time to give up Melton, and hunted in Middlesex, with the King's Staghounds. As I had another daughter in less than another year, I sold a hunter; and before nine years had passed I had seven daughters and a wife I loved dearly, and having each year sold a hunter, I was reduced at last to my brown cob. Now I have my ride to the meet on him, potter about through the best line o' gates I can find, and enjoy life as much as ever." And indeed I well remember Mr. Carroll's round jolly red face, his short curly flaxen hair, his quiet humour and ready wit. His portrait is to be seen in the picture by Grant of the Royal Hunt, in the left-hand corner of it; he is represented without his hat, on a cob, talking to Sir Seymour Blane and his bosom friend, Johnny Bushe, and looking up to him is Paddy, the fellow who used to run with the pack.

Some of Carroll's sayings were very smart. On one occasion, when Lord Adolphus Fitzclarence—who was of course a sailor, the son of our sailor king and the famous actress, Mrs. Jordan—was telling the company after dinner that he had had a bad fall over a fence near Hardwick, Carroll said, "Oh! it could not have hurt you much, as you are too much of *a Tar* to care for *a pitch.*"

CHAPTER VII.

Louis XVIII. at Hartwell—The English Garden—The King has his own again; my Father escorts him to London—The Manners of Parochial Clergy—Tate and Brady triumphant—Horse-whipping a Miller—An Independent Tory—Anecdote of Lord Palmerston and the Witty Bishop.

WHEN Napoleon the Great, at the beginning of this century, drove the Royal Family out of France, and they sought shelter with us, our Government were doubtful where they could be placed in safety, so as to prevent a *coup de main* either from the French themselves, or by the Revolutionary party in England; and it was deemed necessary for their security that the Royal exiles should reside somewhere in the centre of England. Hartwell was the place selected, a stately mansion surrounded with fine timber, standing in a park of great pastoral beauty. A picturesque little church, embosomed in trees, is within a hundred yards of the mansion, with large kitchen gardens and remarkably pleasing ornamental grounds adjoining it, with shady alcoves enclosing a lovely bowling-green, where Louis XVIII. and his small Court were fond of disporting themselves. About the year 1808 they took up their residence at Hartwell, and the resources of the little village were strained to their utmost to accommodate the Court. Every lodge, even the gardeners' and gamekeepers' cottages, were occupied by Royalties or important people attendant on the King. In one small cottage in the wood was housed the Duchesse d'Angoulême; the Duc de Berri in one of the lodges, in another the Duc de Blacas; whilst the King and his amiable consort, with the Prince de Condé, and their personal retinue, occupied the mansion, one of the rooms of which was fitted up as a chapel with confessional, and other rooms for the abbé attendant on his Majesty. The French nobility, with their families, were to be seen visiting the primitive inhabitants of this Buckinghamshire village, and often extended their walks to attend the market at the town of Aylesbury, which stands about two miles distant.

In that town my father had come to reside, when about twenty-one years of age (in 1812), and, wonderful to relate, had already acquired, at Berkhampstead Grammar School, a good knowledge of the French language—a rare accomplishment in those days, when the Continent was practically closed against all but the wealthiest Englishmen—and he was almost the only man in the neighbourhood of Aylesbury who could converse with the Royal Family and their retinue. The King often sent for him on matters of business, and I have heard him tell many anecdotes of the residents of the house, and of the habits there of the French Court. Generally the King, with a certain amount of royal state, dined in public, and people were admitted to walk past the party when at dinner. The French Queen died at Hartwell: after the entrance of the allies into Paris, in 1814, her body was taken to France, and I believe was buried at St. Denis. Portraits of Louis XVIII., "Louis le Desiré," as he was called, are still to be seen in Hartwell House, with the Prince de Condé and other celebrities attached to the retinue of the King. The old churchyard has several memorials of those who died in exile, but I cannot find that any Frenchman or Frenchwoman remained behind when the King for the last time left the village. I have many times in wandering among the shady groves of Hartwell found, carved on the trees, lines giving expression to the sense of comfort and happiness which the exiles experienced during their prolonged stay here; one tree has carved deeply in the bark, "Quel Plaisir"; another beech-tree, "Toujours Heureux."

Louis, on his return to France, had a garden formed and planted at Versailles, on the plan, exactly reproduced, of the Queen's private garden at Hartwell, that he might commemorate, so he said, "the happy, happy days he had spent in that charming county." This garden still exists, but very few of the visitors to the glorious palace of Versailles, who ask for "Le Jardin Anglais," are aware of its origin. During the past twenty years I have twice visited it, but am bound to say, that either the one has been so grown over, or the other at Hartwell has been so altered, that I failed to connect them, except in the general outline and usual character of a truly "English" garden.

JOURNEY TO LONDON.

At Aylesbury great were the rejoicings in 1814, and loud the shoutings when it was announced that the allied armies had entered Paris, that the great Napoleon had signed his abdication, and that "the King would have his own again." The town of Aylesbury was *en fête* as the French King passed through it on his way to London—a narrow street leading into the Market Square still perpetuates the memory of the event by bearing the name of Bourbon Street. My father with five other young men mounted their horses to form a small body-guard and rode by the side of the King's carriage, intending to go as far as the first stage to Great Berkhampstead, about fourteen miles from Hartwell. The King's carriage was drawn by four post-horses, and several other carriages followed. On arriving at Berkhampstead the first change of horses was at the King's Arms, then kept by a Mr. Page, who had three very good-looking daughters, one of whom, sweet Miss Polly—not sweet Anne—Page, the King had often been much struck with; and he never passed through the town either going to or coming from the Metropolis without having a chat and paying attentions to "sweet Polly Page." This was well known to my father and his friends, and they knew therefore that a quarter of an hour or so would be consumed in the ostensible act of changing horses, while the King would devote the time to a flirtation with the fair Polly. They therefore pushed on to Boxmoor, about four miles, gave their horses a mouthful of hay and some water, and waited for the King's arrival, intending to accompany him as far as Watford. His Majesty caught sight of the cavalcade, and expressed to my father the pleasure he felt at their attention. Being well mounted, they trotted on another seven miles to Watford, and there hearing that our Prince Regent, with many of the great officers of State, and several Royal princes from the Continent, were assembled to meet his Majesty at Stanmore, they resolved, if possible, to see this historic interview. Riding on to Bushey, without stopping at Watford, they had time to have their somewhat tired horses groomed down and fed, and by the time the King arrived, four of them—for two could not get further than Boxmoor—were mounted and ready again to continue their escort ; and they thus rode on to the Abercorn Arms at Stanmore. There was a great crowd round the portico of the inn, and a guard of cavalry to receive his Majesty. My father and his three friends pushing forward, the King seemed greatly pleased, and desired them to keep near him. They jumped off their horses and stood on each side of the entrance, and saw the Prince Regent embrace the French King, and receive him with much affection amidst the enthusiasm of the people, which was unbounded. Again mounting their nags, they rode towards London ; within about a mile from London the Royal *cortège* again overtook them, and they accompanied the King to the Pulteney Hotel (I think that was the name), where his retinue were to be accommodated. After seeing the King safely bestowed, my father and his friends rode off, tired enough, to the Old Bell in Holborn, at that time one of the leading inns in London, and which may yet be seen in its primitive state, the galleries round the old stable-yard, the old coffee-room, with box divisions, scarcely altered for 150 years or more.

My father served the office of Vicar's churchwarden for twenty-five years in succession to the Rev. Mr. Morley. Many scenes I can call to recollection, thought innocent enough at the time, of the manners then of the parochial clergy. Aylesbury was a "peculiar," and therefore not under the jurisdiction of the Archdeacon, and once a year "The Peculiar," as he was called, visited the parish, and this visit was made the occasion of a demonstration in favour of the Church, and as a natural consequence then, a jovial dinner followed. I am sorry to say that at such gatherings I have repeatedly seen even the clerical dignitaries themselves in a high state of fever, I fear not so much from their post-prandial speeches, as from the libations they poured out and imbibed in responding to the loyal and patriotic toasts which were given on these occasions. It was the custom for about thirty of the principal inhabitants to dine together, and a sum of £5 or £6 was charged to the parish from the church-rate, the balance being paid *pro rata* by those who dined, and this custom was continued until loud complaints were made, when the question of church-rates became a *vexata quæstio*.

As an instance of the complete change of opinion that has taken place since that time, especially as to the manner of conducting Divine service, I may state that in the old church at Aylesbury, which is one of great beauty and interest—erected about the end of the twelfth century, and a splendid specimen of early English—a huge organ gallery filled up the whole of the centre of the tower and part of the transepts; on each side were seats for the choir—two young ladies usually taking the solos and singing them very artistically, assisted by some six well-trained amateurs with really fine voices. Before the service commenced, a very elaborate piece of music, with an organ accompaniment, more theatrical than devotional, was given; a special favourite was "Sound the Loud Timbrel." Of chanting there was none, but an elaborate anthem was sung, and the new version of the Psalms by Tate and Brady, to be found in all Prayer-books of the time. The old Vicar, Mr. Morley, being at least seventy years of age, married for the second time a young and very pretty woman, who, on coming to the Vicarage, brought about a complete revolution, and introduced a very low church service and an Evangelical style of doctrine, with a hymn-book which was looked upon with the greatest horror by the older members of the congregation. On the old Vicar wishing the new hymn-book to be used, the choir resigned, the organ was played in dumb show, and as soon as one of the newly-introduced hymns were given out, most of the leading families left the church. Dr. Kaye, the Bishop of Lincoln (Aylesbury was then in the Lincoln Diocese), tried to calm down the schism; my father carried on the correspondence on behalf of the parishioners; the trouble ended in a compromise, one old psalm and one hymn being declared the rule in each service. The truce negotiated, the choir returned to their duties; but the breach had been created, and from that date the parish has been divided by very sharp lines, and now the Evangelical party have built a church of their own, in the adjoining hamlet of Walton.

Mr. Morley was succeeded at Aylesbury by the Rev. J. Pretyman, a grand-nephew of the Bishop of Lincoln, and Mr. Pretyman by the Rev. Edward Bickersteth, Archdeacon of Buckingham, afterwards Dean of Lichfield. The Archdeacon, Purey Cust, now the accomplished Dean of York, was the next incumbent, and was followed by the Rev. Arthur Lloyd, now Vicar and Canon of Newcastle-on-Tyne, who is acting Dean of that new diocese, and a most powerful and eloquent preacher. It is curious that three succeeding vicars have been promoted successively to deaneries, and I may safely say that the parochial reign for more than thirty years of three such men has had a great and beneficial effect on the character of the people, their churchmanship, and sense of Christian duties, not only in the town, but in the whole neighbourhood.

When I was about twenty years of age I had already taken a part in the religious politics of the day. The wrangle over church-rates, which had been steadily growing in rancour for some years, had now become intensified, and in no part of England perhaps did the *odium theologicum* rage with greater violence than at Aylesbury. My father had been Vicar's churchwarden for many years, and, like his people before him, had been very persistent in standing up for the rights and privileges of the Church. A big, burly miller, named Pursell, one of the overseers of the parish, took a very prominent part in the opposition to church-rates, and he came up one evening in June to my father, who was standing under the portico in front of his own house, and began abusing him shamefully, and accusing him of malversation of the parish money. My sister, who happened to overhear the conversation, sent for me, as I was enjoying a game of bowls on the bowling-green. By the time I arrived upon the scene I found Mr. Pursell shaking his fist in my father's face, and applying the most abusive epithets to him. I hurried up and told him if he "dared to insult my father I would give him a deuced good horsewhipping." He at once turned his wrath on me, and finally I took my hunting-whip and thrashed him without mercy, while he strove all the time to hit me, but I was far too active for him, and escaped his every onslaught. He soon took himself off, and shortly afterwards brought an action against my father and myself for assault and battery. My father defended the action, and his solicitor engaged the then well-known Serjeant Storks and Mr. Byles (afterwards Mr. Justice Byles) as Junior, who advised that we should plead guilty and admit our liability for damages, and have a jury under the Sheriff to assess them.

The day of trial having come, we found Mr. Fitzroy Kelly, afterwards Lord Chief Baron, and Mr. Roberts arrayed against us. The Court was crowded to suffocation. After the examination of the witnesses for the plaintiff, Mr. Serjeant Storks said he did not intend to call any witnesses, and thus prevented Mr. Kelly addressing the jury in reply. The serjeant made a most humorous and telling speech, and the jury gave a verdict "for the defendants!" for, they said, it served the rascal right, and every one of them would have acted as I had done if they had been in my place. The

Under-sheriff explained to the jury that they had only to assess the damages, and that we had pleaded "guilty." The damages having been claimed as £300, it was for them to say how much of that sum they would assess; but they still persisted in finding for the defendants, and it was not until they had been told that it could not end there, that if they still gave this verdict the case would have to be carried to a higher court, and would cost the defendants a very heavy sum, that they consented to give damages, £5. We had offered £100 to settle it before going to trial, so the result was a great triumph for my father. The trial, however, with costs, came to more than the £100, and the costs to the plaintiff to over £70; so much for thrashing a miller, however abusive!

In connection with the Tate and Brady version of the Psalms, I remember being told a good story, as all stories about Lord Palmerston and Wilberforce, Bishop of Oxford, are likely to be. On one occasion these two were visiting at a country house, and on the morning of departure were told that carriages were ready to take the departing guests to the railway station. Palmerston settled to go in one of these carriages, as he feared there would be rain; but the Bishop, who was a great pedestrian, preferred to walk. Before he had proceeded half-way to the station a heavy storm of rain came on; yet the good Bishop struggled on, when the carriage containing Lord Palmerston overtook him, and his lordship called out from its window a part of the first verse of the Tate and Brady version of the first psalm—

"How blest is he who ne'er consents
By ill advice to walk."

But Bishop Wilberforce, with the usual twinkle in his eye, replied with the remainder of the verse—

"Nor stands in sinners' ways, nor sits
Where men profanely talk."

And the Bishop drew to one side, and proceeded to walk on. As our friends across the Atlantic would say, "The Bishop had him thar!"

Another story used to be told about Bishop Wilberforce, which, authentic or not, was believed to be so in the locality of Aylesbury, and was held to be a righteous illustration of episcopal displeasure at unworthy tale-bearing. An evangelical rector represented to the Bishop that, among other such enormities, a neighbouring broad-church sporting parson actually proposed to ride a match at a county hunt race meeting. "Does he, indeed?" said his amiable Bishop. "Then, I bet half-a-crown he wins."

CHAPTER VIII.

Prison Discipline Fifty Years Ago—Sweeping the Streets of Aylesbury—Old Jem and his Bill—Description of the County Prison—Murderers and their Beer—Attempted Escapes—John Tawell, Quaker; his Trial for Murder and his previous Career —"Apple-pip Kelly"— Imprisonment for Debt — Captain Paulet and "Tally-ho ! Hanmer."

IN recalling my recollections of prison discipline, it seems to me that many of the customs which then appeared ordinary instances of life can scarcely now be credited. Market-day at Aylesbury was Saturday ; and after four o'clock in the afternoon, gangs of prisoners were turned out of the gaol, under the superintendence of one, or at most two, turnkeys, to sweep the streets. These prisoners were dressed in blue and yellow uniforms, cut in grotesque fashion, and carried their birchbrooms with them. Many of their friends from different parts of the county came to see them, and chatted and joked with them in the streets during their scavenging surreptitiously gave them tobacco and money, occasionally treated them with beer, and many a joke was cracked with boisterous laughter. No disgrace was felt at having friends who were convicts, and the inhabitants of the town looked upon it as a good thing to get their streets cleaned at the expense of the country.

In front of the County Hall was a broad footway, fenced on the side of the roadway by thick, iron posts, to which were attached strong chains; from this paved footway the office of the Clerk of the Peace and the Assize Court and Magistrates' Chamber were approached by broad flights of steps. The footway was called the "Gaol Stones," and for the first quarter of the present century the debtors were permitted to exercise here, and to sit on the steps to the court, the public passing and repassing all day being subject to the ribald jokes, and oftentimes insulting speeches, made to them by these, generally dishonest, inhabitants of the debtors' wards. Beer was a luxury often indulged in in full view of the public; but this scandal at last was abolished by order of the magistrates. Prisoners were often employed outside the gaol walls, and Mr. Acton Chaplin, who was for many years Clerk of the Peace, was permitted to use the labour of the prisoners for his own private use. At one time he held about forty acres of the farm I have since occupied, the Prebendal Farm, which adjoined my residence (Willowbank), which then belonged to Mr. A. Chaplin, from whose family I purchased it. The ornamental grounds adjoining the house were extensive and beautiful, high banks planted with fine timber, a lake of nearly an acre in extent, supplied with water from an adjacent mill-stream; and these grounds were all laid out and completed by prisoners from the gaol, and the farm land was cultivated also by the spade husbandry of these men. The gangs were marched across the main street from a back entrance of the county gaol in charge of an old turnkey; and so little degradation did the men feel, and so easy was their lot, that escapes were scarcely even heard of or attempted by men who were sentenced to short terms of imprisonment.

An amusing incident happened to my father when he first came to Aylesbury in 1812. Old Mr. Sheriff, the then governor of the gaol, was an intimate friend of my grandfather's, and he was anxious to assist his friend's son. He offered my father the services of one of the prisoners to do the odd work of the house, such as milking the cow, feeding the pigs, working in the garden, etc., and my father was nothing loth in accepting it. The man, who was undergoing a sentence of six months' hard labour, and had served part of his time, immediately entered on his duties, had his dinner daily and half a pint of beer, and dressed in his labourer's clothes and not in the gaol uniform—was, in fact, treated as one of the servants of the household. My father was seated at his dinner one market-day, at the termination of the prisoner's sentence and after he had had his discharge, when he was told "Jem" wanted to see him. "Come in," said my father; "what is it you want?" "Well, sir," Jem replied, "I've brought in your little bill;" and he handed him a little scrap of paper, made out by himself, charging about 6d. per day for all the days he had been at work. My father said, "What do you mean, you scoundrel? why, you have been a prisoner all the time. If you don't take yourself off my premises directly I'll send the constable after you." Jem took the hint and himself off at the same time, and I suppose went home on his way rejoicing. This is a sample of gaol discipline within easy recollection.

The sons of our neighbour, the governor, being about my own age, and going to the same school, I was constantly visiting at their residence within the walls of the prison, while the windows of our nursery and other rooms looked into the gaol premises. I therefore had many opportunities of seeing the prisoners, and of knowing the system of management then employed. At that time, 1824 to 1840, and for very many years previously, scarcely any attempt at classification of prisoners had been practised; and in this prison, which had the reputation of being excellently managed, there were about eight wards, surrounded by high walls, with loose bricks at the top to crush the rash convict who would venture to escape. Around these wards were the living-rooms; the floor as well as some of the yards were paved with Yorkshire flagstones, a few had a pavement round a gravel centre. There were open fireplaces in most of the rooms, closets, and dust-holes adjoining. The sleeping-rooms over the living-rooms were caged off into separate enclosures by iron bars, with a boarded partition between each cage; the doors were iron gratings with a bar to drop on the staple on the floor, the cage opposite having a similar arrangement, so that two bars might fall on the same staple. Sometimes the turnkey would accidentally omit to thread the chain through one of the staples, or the bar might be bent, and so the prisoner would very often have it in his power to open his door, and the opposite one of course also, and two prisoners would be at large in the room, performing any practical jokes they liked on those who were in the still secured compartments. Such prisoners as were to be tried at the Assizes, and those accused of very heinous crimes, were in close cells, but all opened into one room. The drop or gallows was fixed on an iron balcony running along and fronting the street in advance of the three large centre windows of the County Hall. The first ward was called the Old Gaol, and there those accused of heinous crimes, and those who were to be tried at the Assizes, were confined. Here convicts awaiting the convenience of the authorities for removal for transportation, and murderers, and perpetrators of other terrible crimes who had been acquitted on the ground of insanity, might be seen side by side with some young man of great respectability and good position, afterwards to be proved by trial to be innocent, compelled to associate with wretches like these, and to submit to the fellowship, ribald conversation, or blasphemy of the vilest and most hardened criminals. Then came the New Gaol for those of lesser crimes, awaiting trial at Quarter Sessions; then the Datchet Ward, named after a number of rioters from the village of that name once incarcerated here; and next came the Women's Ward. There were two larger wards called the Bridewell, for men undergoing various terms of imprisonment, and below these were the Boys' Wards; then the chapel, adjoining which was the Debtors' Ward; and lastly the infirmary.

This system of herding all classes of prisoners together was eminently adapted for the formation of a criminal class, and to that end succeeded admirably.

In the outer doors of these wards I have enumerated was a smaller trap-door, through which various things could be passed to the inmates; and an old woman, Polly Batt, had the privilege of supplying any prisoner with whatever he required, if only he had the money to pay. Tobacco, chops, bacon, vegetables, tea and sugar, could be had, and as scarcely any supervision was exercised, on many occasions files and other implements to aid an escape were surreptitiously conveyed to the inmates. But the crowning absurdity of all remains to be mentioned—these prison worthies were allowed as much beer (but no spirits) as they could pay for; it is true that there was a sort of arrangement that no man should have more than a pint a day, but as a man who had plenty of money could arrange with others who had none, one man might get six or eight pints a day. When the agricultural or Swing rioters were in gaol, in the year 1831, there were served in one day from the White Hart 112 quarts of beer to the various wards. The White Hart was celebrated for its Marlow beer, and it was carried round openly by a potman, who served his customers through the little door, the money being taken at the time, or, if there were any well-known man in gaol, he could go on credit. In an old account-book now before me, I see several items for beer scored up— C. Lynn, 1s.; C. Lynn, 1s. 4d., etc. This man was guilty of a dreadful murder in the Whaddon Chase, but was acquitted on the ground of insanity, and eventually died in the prison, where he was always considered perfectly sane.

When I was a very little boy I remember being taken into the gaol to see some condemned criminals, accompanying my father and several of his friends. We visited Banks and the two Cribbs, under sentence of death for horse-stealing; they were heavily ironed with chains round their ankles, tied up to their waists with a handkerchief. They were notorious thieves, the first of whom acknowledged that he had stolen ninety-nine horses at various times. They were confined in the Old Gaol, the sleeping-cells of which were under the floor of the Assize Courts. These men effected their escape from prison in a very remarkable manner. By some means they possessed themselves of a piece of iron hoop, which they had notched and transformed into a sort of saw; with this and a pocket-knife they managed to peck down the ceiling of their dormitories, and carried away the dislodged plaster in their handkerchiefs each morning and threw it down the drains; they then sawed through the beams and rafters overhead, using great labour and perseverance until they managed to saw through the flooring and obtained an entrance to the Assize Court. One of the Cribbs was a broad-shouldered stout man, and they were more than an hour lifting him through the hole, lacerating his shoulders very much in the operation. From the courts they entered the County Hall adjoining, where they found a long ladder then being used in white-washing the ceiling; they thrust the end of the ladder through one of the windows opening into the Market Square, and from the top spar they tied their sheets and blankets, ripped up into lengths and made into a rope, and by this means they descended into the Square. It was late in the month of February, and, favoured by the darkness, they commenced their descent soon after five in the morning. An old barber, however, named Tommy Norris, who was a very early riser, looking out of his house, which was nearly opposite the County Hall, saw them in the glimmer of the early morning descend the rope. He gave the alarm, the men were followed, and one of the Cribbs was captured on my farm, his fettered legs having caught on the top of a field-gate; he had fallen head-foremost to the ground, where he lay unable to get up. Banks was found in a hayrick about four miles away, and the other condemned felon was captured not far from his comrade in a ditch. They expressed their belief that if they had not been detained so long in getting their comrade through the hole they might have made their escape in safety, even though in irons, as it was no uncommon thing for the gipsies and wandering vagrants to file through prisoners' fetters, and as they had no distinctive clothes, they thus easily would avoid detection.

They were hung according to their sentence. Their companions under sentence of death were Randell and Croker, who had committed a dastardly murder on a poor defenceless old couple named Needle, who kept a turnpike-gate about two miles from Aylesbury, and who were murdered under the impression that they had plenty of money, the takings of a week or more. The wretches found after the murder that the money upon the old people amounted to only a few shillings, as the day before they had remitted the monthly earnings to the lessee of the tolls. The custom at the time I speak of was to hang murderers forty-eight hours after they were sentenced—they were generally tried on Friday that they might be hanged on the Monday morning, giving them a Sunday for a funeral sermon to be preached to them by the chaplain of the gaol—and these three criminals, who had made so gallant a dash for life and liberty, were brought back to prison and hanged *secundem artem*.

Escapes from the gaol at Aylesbury were frequent, and one especially was very boldly planned, and, if it had not been discovered in time, would have led to most serious consequences. One afternoon my father was startled at seeing Mr. Sheriff, the governor, rushing into his house, begging him to come to the gaol with all the men he could collect, as he was afraid the turnkey would be overpowered and half the prisoners in the gaol would escape. At once from all parts of the premises our men were marched off into the prison, armed with a weapon of some kind, an old flint blunderbuss, a ship's cutlass, or a thick stick. The prisoners in the ward called the Old Gaol, the most desperate of the criminals, headed by a young man named Saunders, who was accused of a burglary with violence, with more than twenty horse and sheep stealers, highway robbers, and burglars under his command, were in possession of the ward, and having taken out the wooden legs of the forms and torn up their bedding to make a sort of binding cord to thread the forms together into a ladder, were scaling up the back of the governor's house and into three dormer-windows of the servants' bedrooms, which opened on to a gutter over the gaol-yard. When Mr. Sheriff came into his house, he, with his eldest son, both courageous men, rushed up-stairs, and on going into the attics found Saunders had reached the top and was already in the gutter, while three or four other men were swarming up the impromptu ladder, and would soon have been alongside of their leader. Young Mr. Sheriff grappled with the leader, took him by the collar, and attempted to drag him in through the window, when the scoundrel, finding his case hopeless, determined to kill both himself and his captor at once, and, seizing Mr. Sheriff by his coat-collar, tried to spring over the low parapet down on to the paving-stones below; and thus would have dashed himself and Mr. Sheriff to pieces. Fortunately he slipped into the gutter half over the ledge, and hung almost in mid-air till some warders managed by main force to drag both men into the room through the window. Saunders still fought most stubbornly, but was at length overpowered and secured with strong handcuffs and fetters.

In the meantime, by vigorously pelting those on the temporary ladder and those below with brick-bats, the mutiny was overcome and order restored. It was believed that Charlie Lynn, the Whaddon Chase murderer, had given private information of the intended outbreak to the governor, but had not known how soon it would be attempted. Saunders, who was a good-looking young man of about twenty-four years of age, had been a valet and gentleman's servant, and was tempted and led into evil by bad companions and gay living. He was convicted to be hung for the burglary of which he was accused, and before his execution confessed his crime and gave information about his companions in the burglary, and in consequence another man, named Dowsett, was taken and tried at the next Assizes, found guilty, condemned to death, but afterwards reprieved and sent to Botany Bay for life; there, however, he assaulted one of his keepers, and finally suffered the same fate as Saunders.

There were several remarkable criminal trials in the county of Bucks, and of one of them, at which I was present, I am tempted to give a slight account.

I know few trials of modern times which created greater interest than that of John Tawell, the Quaker, for the murder of Sarah Hart, of Salt Hill. The prisoner was a man of considerable property, who lived at Berkhampstead, and moved in good society. The trial lasted for three days, and was presided over by Baron Park, afterwards Lord Wensleydale. The facts which came out in evidence were these. Sarah Hart was the mother of two children, and lived in a neat little cottage by the side of the high-road at Salt Hill; every quarter-day, or about that time, she used to tell her neighbours she expected her "good man" to call and bring her quarterly income. In the October previous to the murder he had been taken seriously ill after his visit, and so it was with much anxiety she was awaiting him to call in January. She and her children met him at the door; he sent out for some bottled porter for their dinner, and stayed some time. He was seen to leave the cottage very hurriedly, and a violent and shrill scream being heard shortly after his departure, the poor woman's neighbour entered Sarah Hart's cottage and found her in the throes of death. After two or three more screams, one fainter than the other, she expired in her neighbour's arms, on the floor of the cottage.

The affair was so sudden, the woman who was with Mrs. Hart was so unnerved, that the Quaker was not followed. After he left the cottage he hurried towards Slough, met an omnibus going to Windsor, entered it, and, after going rather over half a mile, got out, and was seen by the driver to go up to the house called " The Herschells," which was at one time the residence of the celebrated astronomer, Herschell ; he did not, however, attempt to call, but merely went to the door of the house and turned back again, the omnibus having gone out of sight. He then quickly returned to Slough station, got into a train which was waiting, and was whisked off, as he thought, safely to London. But he had reckoned without his host ; for unknown to him, or at all events unheeded, science had just discovered how to put into practice one of her greatest wonders, the " electric telegraph," this being the first time the invention was put into play as a detective of crime. The stationmaster wired to Paddington—" A Quaker in the train ; watch him, follow him, and on no account lose sight of him ; find out who he is." This was done. Tawell, arriving in town, was followed to a house at Islington, which he entered, and in which he remained for some time. On leaving he was traced to Euston Station, then by rail to Great Berkhampstead, where it was found that he was a well-known and greatly-respected resident. He had been married only two or three years previously to a very charming widow, a Quakeress of the name of Cutforth, living in good style and in high repute. The next day Tawell was arrested, brought to Aylesbury, and at the March Assizes was tried for the murder.

The above facts were proved, and also that he had brought prussic acid at a chemist's shop in London; that the woman Sarah Hart had been his first wife's servant when he was living at Sydney, New South Wales, and that he had two children by her; that he allowed her fifty-two pounds a year, which he paid quarterly; that he wanted not only to save this annual sum, but that he feared daily that she might find out where he lived, and would expose and degrade him amongst all the Friends.

The trial was made memorable by the ingenious and yet preposterous defence set up by his counsel, Mr. Fitzroy Kelly, Q.C., afterwards Lord Chief Baron of the Exchequer. Contrary to experience, there was no smell of prussic acid either in the victim's throat or in the room, and only a faint trace in the intestines. Mr. Kelly therefore hoped to persuade the jury that this trace was the result of her having eaten several apples during the day, which was not denied, some apple-pips being found in the stomach; that all apple-pips contained traces of prussic acid, and would fully account for the small quantity of that deadly poison found in the body. This defence earned for the eminent lawyer the sobriquet of "Apple-pip Kelly." He made a most powerful and eloquent appeal to the jury; and the judge, as it was past six o'clock on the second day, decided to postpone his summing-up till the next day, feeling that a serious impression had been made on the jury, and being determined that they should form a calm decision on this singular case. The next day some witnesses were called to testify to character, the counsel for the prosecution replied on the defence, the judge summed up, and it was again late in the day when the jury retired to consider their verdict. About nine o'clock they returned with a verdict of "Guilty," and Tawell was condemned to death. This seemed quite to astound the prisoner, who had firmly believed he would be acquitted.

The prisoner's version of the case was that he called on the dead woman to pay her as usual her quarterly allowance, and had told her he must leave her never to see her again; that she then took a phial from her pocket and said, "I will do for myself"; he tried to stop her, but she said, "I will, I will," and before he could arrest her hand, she swallowed the poison, and he was so horrified that he got away as fast as he could. But no trace of a phial was found in the room. The excuse the prisoner made for buying prussic acid in London was that he was troubled with varicose veins; and this was true, and he used the same remedy while in prison. His wife firmly believed in his innocence, and, indeed, some of his friends had come down in a carriage from Berkhampstead to bring him home after his acquittal. After his condemnation his poor suffering wife came to visit him, and I escorted her to see her husband. I shall never forget her sorrow and heart-broken grief, nor the appearance of the wretched man. As I entered the parlour of the governor's house, where the interview was to take place, he came in with his warder through another door. He seemed completely paralyzed at the sight of his wife, and turned deadly pale; a poor, insignificant little man in his Quaker's garb, looking utterly miserable. This lady bore her husband one child, a boy, whom she named after his father. Although urged to give him her widowed name of Cutforth, she sternly refused, and to the end she believed in her husband's innocence.

Tawell was hung on a cold March morning; the snow laid thickly on the ground, and the wind swept a driving sleet against the upturned faces of the thousands of people—many of them, I am sorry to say, women—who thronged the Market Square at Aylesbury; and when the bolt was drawn, the wind so buffeted about the wretched little body of the murderer, that it was believed by many he was struggling still for half an hour afterwards. Calcraft, the executioner, however, declared that the man died instantly.

Tawell's confession had been given by him to the Rev. Mr. Cox, the chaplain of the prison, who, however, refused to disclose its contents, saying it was given under the seal of confession to a priest, a course of action that at the time was severely criticized.

Mr. Sheriff, the governor of the gaol, stated that the accused man had actually confessed his guilt the night before his execution, admitting that he had administered the poison in the bottled porter, and that he had made the like attempt in the October previous with morphia, but without success. He further led Mr. Sheriff to believe that he had also tried to poison his son's widow on the same evening at Islington, having ordered bottled

K

porter there also for supper, but her mother would not allow her to drink it. He was an accomplished villain, who made a religious exterior a cloak to his abominable crimes.

Tawell's life was a curious one; he had been apprenticed to a chemist, and afterwards obtained a situation in the house of Marsden and Sons, wholesale druggists, where he became a model assistant, was put on the road as traveller, and whilst thus employed he forged and uttered a cheque on the Uxbridge Bank of Hull and Co., who were also Quakers. At that time forgery was a capital offence, and as the Quakers were averse to taking away life, it was arranged that the criminal should plead guilty to uttering the cheque, but not to forging, and he was sentenced to be transported for fourteen years. He was sent to Sydney, where his wife and family followed him. From his good conduct he soon obtained a ticket-of-leave, and set up a chemist's shop in Sydney, and there rapidly obtained a fortune. His wife died, under suspicious circumstances, of course. Obtaining a free pardon, he returned to England, Sarah Hart accompanying the family; and hence the cottage at Salt Hill and the two children. Married to Mrs. Cutforth, Tawell was anxious to be reinstated in the brotherhood of the Society of Friends, but, fearful of his liaison being discovered, resolved to be rid of Sarah Hart. He was a sordid wretch into the bargain; as he had to pay his son's widow £50 a year, he tried to put her out of the way in the same manner. There is little that is heroic about most criminals.

Imprisonment for debt often struck me as a very bar-

IMPRISONMENT FOR DEBT.

barous custom. If a man got into debt, oftentimes by misfortunes over which he had no control, the law locked him up for an indefinite time, thus preventing him from working or carrying on any business to enable him ever to pay his debts. Some singular illustrations of the folly of the system were given at Aylesbury. A Captain Paulet, brother to Lady Nugent, who had a fine old estate, but from youthful folly and extravagance had got into debt, was imprisoned in the county gaol. He did not approve of the prison fare, and begged my father to supply him daily with breakfast and dinner, half a pint of port wine, and a pint of beer. The Captain remained in prison for over two years, and the account, for which my father received no money at the time, increased to over £150; but my father had confidence in the Captain's honour, and it was justified, for many years afterwards he sent £100, with a promise to pay the balance with interest. Whilst in prison many friends visited the debtor and supplied him with spare cash, till after several years he came into his estate at Addington. But by then he was a broken-down man, and ended his days in an asylum, never having recovered his incarceration. My father did not receive the balance of his account, but I have no doubt, had the Captain been able to have legally arranged with his creditors, most of them would have been paid, at all events a reasonable composition, and he might have ended his days as a quiet country gentleman.

I remember Captain Paulet well; he had been a great fisherman, and once caught the finest pike I ever saw from the Weston Turville reservoir; it was in splendid condition, and weighed twenty-eight and a half pounds. The Captain sent it as a present to the market-table at the White Hart; it was baked on a board, no tin or dish being long enough. I took out the teeth, and for many years used them as cribbage-pegs. Captain Paulet's estate was in the end purchased by the Right Hon. J. Gellibrand Hubbard, afterwards raised to the peerage as Baron Addington.

Another odd occupant of the debtors' prison, some time afterwards, was an eccentric country parson, the rector of Simpson, in the county of Bucks. He was of good family, and rejoiced in the name of "Tally-ho! Hanmer," a reckless fox-hunting parson, of not much credit to his cloth. I never saw this amiable cleric in any other costume than mahogany-coloured top-boots and a square-cut black riding-coat, with black breeches, crowned by a peculiar low black hat, with a broad and flat brim. When "Tally-ho! Hanmer" was in very low water, he would borrow a sovereign or a five-pound note, with garnished tale of great distress, from many an old college friend. On one occasion a generous individual, touched by a sad story of his, forked out a five-pound note to enable the lively rector to go home to his Buckinghamshire parish to perform his Sunday duties. The donor told a mutual friend of mine and his of his action, and was astonished to hear that he had been fleeced. They were both going to dine at Long's Hotel in Bond Street, and on entering the passage—there, not to be mistaken, hung Parson Hanmer's hat! They entered the coffee-room, the impecunious rector was there, supplied with a most *recherché*

IMPRISONMENT FOR DEBT.

dinner and a bottle of champagne at his elbow, spending the five pounds kindly lent him to go home to his duties. He brazened the situation out, finished his repast, wished his friend good-night, and went on to the play.

This frolicsome parson owed my father about £190 for food supplied to him in prison. My father never was paid a farthing of it. He was popular in his parish with all his faults, charitable to the poor, and, I have been told, preached excellent sermons. His rectory house was generally barricaded against creditors throughout the week, and only on Sundays could he walk about in its grounds and visit his parishioners.

These were men of the past. "Tally-ho! Hanmer" was a rollicking jolly sportsman, a bachelor, and a type of a class once very prevalent in England. For good or evil such men are no more.

CHAPTER IX.

The "Rochester Room" at the White Hart, Aylesbury—Its Decoration and History—The Glories of Eythrope—Sir Walter Scott—Vernon's Anecdotes about Turner—Anecdotes of Landseer—"Swill" from Her Majesty's Kitchens—Charles Gow—A Pun and its Interpretation by *Punch*.

AMONGST our most interesting of popular antiquities are our ancient English mansions, their halls and libraries, and surroundings. It is much to be deplored that authentic records of these fast-disappearing landmarks of our own national history have not more often been preserved. The "Old Room" is an example of such a landmark, most interesting in relation to the event whose memory it was built to perpetuate, and most curious in respect to its appearance. But the "Old Rochester Room" at Aylesbury is now only a memory; the site of the once well-known hostelry, the White Hart, is now covered by the Corn Exchange and public markets. The building, at the time of its demolition, was in a most substantial state of preservation, and the "Old Room," with its pictures, and elaborate gilding and ornamentation, had only been lately cleaned and restored, and looked, as it really was, in 1864, in as good trim as the day it left the hands of the builder and decorator.

This room was forty-two feet by twenty-three, and twelve feet in height; it was panelled from top to bottom with recesses in solid framework finely carved for the reception of paintings; the "egg and tongue" ornament in carved wood ran round the cornice, which was richly gilt; and the spacious fireplace was superbly carved with scroll-work after the fashion of the period, and was also ornamented with gold and other colours. The upper portion of the panelling was arranged with alternate groups of fruit, flowers, and warlike trophies. The ceiling was divided into nine compartments, with gilt bosses at the intersection of the beams. The centre, or largest compartment, was filled with a painting on canvas of two life-sized figures seated, representing Peace and Concord, with palm branches in their hands (the initials C. R. are above the principal figures), and Cherubim flying from behind the clouds, of whom two are bearing a crown, and two are below, holding a scroll with the following legend—

> "Let Peace and Concord sit and singe,
> And Subjects yield obedience to their Kinge."

The other compartments were filled with frescoes, and in the four corners were really artistic emblems of the four seasons. The panelled walls were intended to represent a statue and picture gallery; the niches contained painted figures of Julius and Augustus Cæsar, Diana, Juno, Venus, Industry, Diligence, Pallas, Honour, and Majesty; the principal compartment a large picture on canvas of Æneas carrying his father, Anchises, on his shoulder from the burning Troy; Creusa was seated on the ruins, and "The boy, Ascanius," was depicted looking up at his father. This was a copy of the Vatican picture. Over the fireplace was a picture of Tomyris, Queen of the Scythians, receiving the head of the great Cyrus, which she had ordered to be thrown into a vessel of human blood, after she had defeated and killed him, with the words, "Satia te sanguine quem semper sitisti." Two other large paintings filled the remaining compartments, representing Mercury and Argus; and over the door was a recumbent Venus with a Cupid holding back the drapery—a grand picture in life-size. The grate was brought from a house built for Nell Gwynne by Charles II., and was a peculiarly handsome one. On a gable outside the room was the date in large iron figures, 1663.

The circumstances under which this room in the White Hart was built are these. Clarendon, in his *History of the Great Rebellion*, relates that—

"When he (Rochester) returned from the north he lodged at Aylesbury; and having been observed to ride out of the way in a large ground, not far from the town, of which he seemed to take some survey, and had asked many questions of a country fellow who was there (that ground in truth belonging to his own wife), the next Justice of the Peace had notice of it; who, being a man devoted to the Government, and all that country very ill affected always to the King, and the news of Salisbury and the proclamation thereupon having put all men on their guard, came himself to the town where the Earl was; and being informed that there were only two gentlemen above at supper (for Sir Nicholas Armorer was likewise with the Earl, and had accompanied him in that journey), he went into the stable; and upon view of the horses, found they were the same which had been observed in the ground. The Justice commanded the keeper of the inn, one Gilvy, who, besides that he was a person notoriously affected to the Government, was likewise an officer, 'That he should not suffer those horses, nor the persons to whom they belonged, to go out of the honse, till he, the said Justice, came thither in the morning, when he would examine the gentlemen, who they were, and from whence they came.' The Earl was quickly advertised of all that passed below, and enough apprehensive of what must follow in the morning. Whereupon he presently sent for the master of the house, and nobody being present but his companion, he told him, 'He would put his life into his hands, which he might destroy or preserve: that he could get nothing by the one, but by the other he should have profit, and the goodwill of many friends, who might be able to do him good.' Then he told him who he was; and as an earnest of more benefit that he might receive hereafter, he gave him thirty or forty Jacobus's, and a fair gold chain, which was more worth to be sold than one hundred pounds. Whether the man was moved by the reward, which he might have possessed without deserving it, or by generosity, or by wisdom and foresight, for he was a man of very good understanding, and might consider the changes which followed after, and in which this service proved of advantage to him, he did resolve to permit and contrive their escape. And though he thought fit to be accountable to the Justice for their horses, yet he caused two other, as good for their purpose, of his own, to be made ready by a trusty servant in another stable; who about midnight conducted them into London-way, which put them in safety. The innkeeper was visited in the morning by the Justice, whom he carried into the stable where the horses still stood, he having still kept the key in his own pocket, not making any doubt of the persons while he kept their horses; but the innkeeper confessed they were escaped out of the house in the night, how or whither he could not imagine. The Justice threatened loud; but the innkeeper was of that unquestionable fidelity, and gave such daily demonstration of his affection to the Commonwealth, that Cromwell more suspected the connivance of the Justice (who ought not to have deferred the examination of the persons till the morning) than the integrity of a man so well known as the innkeeper was. The Earl remained in London whilst the inquiry was warm and importunate, and afterwards easily procured a passage for Flanders, and so returned to Cologne."

Tradition, borne out by many facts, then records that after the year 1660, when Charles II. was restored to the throne, Gilvy, the innkeeper mentioned in this history, was sent for to Court, and the King paid him great attention, for he had then become a colonel in the army of the Commonwealth; and that the Earl of Rochester, out of gratitude to him for saving his life, came down to Aylesbury, and, as a lasting memorial of his escape and of his gratitude, built him this room and appurtenances, and decorated it as here described.

Many persons who were good judges of pictures consider they were all painted by Antonio Verrio, who painted the ceilings at Whitehall; at all events, no expense had been spared to render the building worthy of the event it was built to commemorate.

The White Hart is supposed by many to have been an inn as far back as the Wars of the Roses, and to have been the rendezvous of the White Rose Party. The old structure, which was pulled down in 1813, was a very curious building, with three high gables facing the street, and a large gallery running round the great court-yard. There was one singular circumstance relating to it, in the names of the rooms on the ground floor, which names were retained until the house was pulled down for the Corn Exchange in 1863. The commercial-room kept its name of "Change"—it was where, in the remembrance of many old people, the principal business of the town was carried on; "The Crown," where the taxes and customs were collected; "The Mitre," where the Church dues were annually paid; and "The Fountain," a name often used in connection with inns or taverns, but the meaning of which is somewhat obscure. It is stated that the Bishops of Lincoln, in whose diocese Aylesbury then was, held their visitations uninterruptedly at the White Hart for nearly three centuries. Every one who knew the old house deeply regretted its destruction, but, like many other buildings, it has yielded to the necessities of modern requirements, and the handsome Corn Exchange and the commodious markets now stand where it once stood, and probably will be of as much service to future generations as the old inn was to thousands who took their ease therein, and who each in his turn have departed out of this world. But the old motto seems like to be forgot—

"Let Peace and Concord sit and singe,
And Subjects yield obedience to their Kinge."

Eythrope House, about four miles from the town of Aylesbury, at the beginning of the present century was a splendid residence, and the then Earl of Chesterfield kept great state there. The park, gardens, and ornamental grounds covered several score of acres around the house, and a large sheet of water, well stocked with fish, added greatly to the beauty of the view from the mansion, and formed a charming feature in the landscape. The house was approached by a classic bridge of ornamental stonework, flanked on either side with statues of great size and elegance. This noble mansion is also a thing of the past; it was pulled down and utterly destroyed in the year 1812.

A curious story was accepted in Aylesbury to account for the destruction of Eythrope, and the retirement of the family of the Chesterfields from the neighbourhood. It was told me by one who was a resident near Eythrope at the time, and who vouched for its truth. About the beginning of the century the Earl of Chesterfield was confidently expecting to receive the appointment of Lord-Lieutenant of the County, the then occupant of the post, a very old man, being reported to be dying. A distinguished party was visiting at Eythrope at the time; the Earl and most of his guests had been amusing themselves in the morning, riding and shooting, but returned to the house for luncheon. One gentleman who had remained indoors, and received first inspection of the mid-day post-bag, greeted his host with, "Halloa, Chesterfield; here's startling news," and proceeded to read from the daily paper an account of the death of the Lord-Lieutenant of Buckinghamshire, in which it was stated also that the Prime Minister, William Pitt, had already promised Baron Cobham the now vacant Lord-Lieutenancy. The brow of the expectant Lord-Lieutenant was clouded, he retired to his room, and begged to be excused appearing at dinner that evening; the next morning he said he had important business in town, which required his immediate attention. The house party broke up and rapidly dispersed. Lord

Chesterfield left Eythrope that day, and never set foot again in the county. A year or two after he gave orders that the mansion should be destroyed and the place dismantled, and the glories of Eythrope came to an end.

The Eythrope estate subsequently became the property of the Marquis d'Harcourt; from him it was purchased a few years since by Miss Alice de Rothschild, who has built a spacious pavilion near the site of the old house, and has once more made the gardens celebrated for artistic design and their beautiful display of flowers and rare shrubs.

My recollection does not, of course, carry me back to the time when Lord Chesterfield entertained men of fashion and fame at Eythrope, but still it seems able to transport me to days distant enough for the thoughts of ordinary men and their methods of life to be very different to what they are now. I remember one evening, in the year 1828, a carriage and pair of horses pulling up at our door, and a benevolent-looking, elderly gentleman, with a young lady, alighting therefrom to take up their abode for the night; after they had dined and retired to bed, a servant informed my father that he had learned from the servant in attendance upon the visitor that his master was "Mister" Walter Scott. My father at once knew, from the portraits he had seen of the author of *Waverley*, who his illustrious guest must be, and told me to wait with my mother and younger brother in the hall to wish the guest of the night good morning—we were youngsters then of six or seven years. I remember Sir Walter, as he thanked my father for his attention to him and his daughter. My father answered, "That if Sir Walter had had a hundredth part of the entertainment that the perusal of his charming writings had given to himself, he would indeed have been pleased." Sir Walter, shaking my father by the hand, warmly thanked him for his expressions of appreciation, and patted me on the head, saying he hoped I should grow up to be a good man; then his daughter kissed me, and the carriage rolled on to its destination.

Some years ago I was very intimate with Vernon Heath, who achieved great success as a photographic artist, not only in portraiture, but chiefly in his magnificent studies of trees and landscape scenery. Vernon Heath was a nephew of Mr. Robert Vernon, who bequeathed his wonderful collection of pictures of British art to the nation. I occasionally visited at Mr. Vernon's residence, at 50, Pall Mall, and heard several anecdotes relating to him and his pictures. One of his best pictures was by his friend Turner, the *Golden Branch* I think it is called; in the foreground there is a female figure with a sickle in her hand. This picture was placed over the mantel-piece in the breakfast-room, and one morning Vernon Heath remarked to his uncle "that the figure was moving." The owner laughed and made light of it, but next morning Vernon Heath again said, "I am sure it is moving and has moved"; with that he mounted some steps and discovered that the figure had curled up and was nearly detached from the picture. Old Mr. Vernon, in a rage, summoned Turner at once. When the great artist arrived, he coolly got on to the steps, and with his fingers pulled the figure off the picture. He then allayed Mr. Vernon's wrath by explaining that he remembered the circumstance well, that he had cut out the figure in paper, stuck it on casually, and went on painting over it, forgetful of the fact; and, although some years had elapsed since the picture was painted, no effect had been produced on it until probably the warmth of the fireplace had at last curled it up. Turner at once repaired the damage, and the canvas is none the worse for it.

One of the most charming pictures ever painted by Landseer, which is by many connoisseurs thought to be his best in the Vernon selection, is that of the two King Charles spaniels lying on a table, with a cavalier's hat and plume near them, and a few other accessories. The history, as related to me by Vernon Heath, is amusing. Mr. Vernon had given Landseer a commission to paint a picture to be exhibited the following year at the British Institution, which was next door to his residence; the price was to be 500 guineas, the subject being left to Landseer, who chose some of his patron's noted King Charles spaniels, and took sketches accordingly. The day for receiving the pictures arrived, the post of honour over the fireplace in the principal room being reserved for Landseer, but no picture was forthcoming, the excuse being that pressure of business had prevented its completion. Next year again, and some weeks before the opening, Vernon Heath called to remind the artist of his promise, and on the day for receiving the works of art exactly the same thing occurred, and no "Landseer" was exhibited. This excited Vernon's ire, but there was no help for it, and with renewed promises for the next season his wrath was appeased. Determined not to be thrice disappointed, Vernon Heath was sent to the dilatory painter in good time, and, to his disgust, there was apparently no picture ready, but two days only before the reception Landseer promised faithfully it should be in the place reserved for it. As several considerable advances of money had been made by Mr. Vernon on the strength of his promises, he insisted that no failure should again occur, and on the morning before the opening the picture arrived quite wet from the easel. Vernon Heath assured me that it had not been commenced more than forty-eight hours before its delivery! When the picture is carefully examined, every one will be perfectly astonished at the marvellous dexterity and beauty of finish of this masterly performance—£500 was thus easily and satisfactorily earned in less than two days.

Landseer often told the following story of himself, which was related to me by the Duke of Grafton, when still Lord Charles Fitzroy. He was once passing down a street near Piccadilly, and seeing a very good specimen of his own work in the window of a picture-dealer, walked into the shop and inquired the name of the painter. The attendant said the picture was a genuine Landseer, and one of the best he ever painted. Landseer took it up and critically examined it, and asked if the dealer could warrant it. "Most certainly," he replied; "and what is more, he'll never paint another." "How is that?" says Landseer. "Gone, sir, gone," he replied, putting his finger to his forehead; "gone, sir, completely off his head, and not likely ever to recover." Landseer, splitting with laughter, hurried out of the shop, fearing he might hear more of his supposed infirmity. Lord Charles Fitzroy told me another characteristic story of Landseer in connection with one of his most noted pictures, that of a boat crossing a loch in Scotland, containing portraits of the late Prince Albert and her Majesty, with gillies in attendance, returning from a shooting excursion. This picture was being painted at Balmoral, and the Prince was particularly anxious that the portrait of the Queen should be correct; Landseer indeed had painted it in and out several times. One morning early, Prince Albert entered the studio before Landseer was up, and found the Queen's portrait admirably delineated, and he immediately wrote on a half sheet of paper, which he fixed to the easel, "Portrait of the Queen excellent and highly satisfactory." Some time afterwards, on entering the studio, he found Landseer had smudged and painted out the likeness to show that he was not to be interfered with or dictated to by any one. Landseer was quick at catching likenesses; once, when he was on a visit to Ardington, Mr. Vernon's country seat in Berkshire, he was asked on coming out of church, "Who preached?" He immediately took out his pencil and sketched on the back of a letter a very correct portrait of the rector, and replied, "I don't know who he was, but that is he." So lifelike was it, that no one who knew the subject could mistake it.

A really clever artist, at the time not much appreciated, Charles Gow, who occasionally exhibited at the Academy, told me an amusing anecdote of one of Landseer's models, a great brawny fellow, who often did duty as one of his Highland keepers; he was a sort of costermonger in London, who somewhere or other kept pigs. One day, when Landseer was painting him, he said, "Mr. Landseer, you be often along o' the Queen; I wish you'd ask a favour of her for me." "What is it?" says Landseer; "perhaps she might grant it." "Well, sir, you see I keeps a pig, and I should be very much obliged to her if she'll let me have her swill." "Swill" in the country we call "hog-wash," the washings-up of the kitchen. Gow, who told me this story, was once painting the portrait of a pony of mine as it was standing in a stall at the White Hart. He was very busy—easel up, maul-stick in hand, palette on thumb, very intently looking at his model. A country labourer opened the door and looked in; he shut it quickly, with an apologetic remark, "Oh, 'scuse me, I see you be a-singeing of him!"

Many of us in our day have sent contributions to that most facetious and clever of all modern publications, *Punch*. Not many of us have seen them appear. Some forty years ago, whilst chatting with a bevy of young friends and manufacturing many wretched puns, I at last hit upon a conundrum which so tickled my companions' risible faculties and mine own, that I proudly sent it to *Punch*. The escape of Louis Napoleon from the fortress of Ham was the constant subject of conversation; my conundrum, "Why did Louis Napoleon *cut away* from Ham?" Answer: "To save his bacon." We young men looked anxiously for the publication of this masterpiece. It appeared; but what was my horror to see it appear, as near as I can remember, thus: "An old gentleman, who has just commenced punning, has sent us the following—'Why did Louis Napoleon cut away from Ham? To save *his bacon.*' The pun is supposed to consist of the connection between *Ham* and *Bacon!*" Here was a miserable ending to all our anticipations; but the editor really thought he had got hold of a good thing, as in the ensuing year's almanac appeared, "On this day Louis Napoleon cut away from Ham to save his bacon"—*Sic transit gloria mundi.*

CHAPTER X.

The Railway Mania—George Hudson, the Railway King—Serving Notices in Ireland—Railway Enterprise and Landlords—George Stephenson and the "Eldest Child"—In Coaching Days—Old Times in Winter—Dr. Lee's Prophecies and their Fulfilment—The late Duke of Buckingham and Chandos: an Uphill Fight—Stowe in Days of Prosperity—The Queen's Visit—In Days of Adversity—Sir Thomas Aubrey as an Upright Judge—Sir John Aubrey and his Dinners for the Free and Independent.

IN our days, when the country is covered with a network of railway lines, some record from personal observations of the great railway mania of 1846-47 may be of some interest. In the previous year Sir Robert Peel, then Prime Minister, had given his vote in favour of direct through lines, and consequently of shorter routes. This stimulated engineers, lawyers, financiers, and a whole troop of company promoters to concoct and bring out schemes for easier access to various points, some of them undoubtedly useful, but many of them utterly impracticable. The Stock Exchange was soon flooded with prospectuses, speculation became rife, and immense fortunes were rapidly made, and, *more suo*, in the end more rapidly dissipated. The name of George Hudson, the "Railway King," recalls to the minds of the older among us the history of the movement. Mr. Hudson, who was a draper in the City of York and Lord Mayor of that ancient city, was connected with the North-Eastern Line, of which he became chairman; and, being a man of real financial ability and determined courage, he rapidly became associated with many of the projected undertakings, notably with the Great Eastern, then called the Eastern Counties Railway. He pushed these forward, and became chairman of some of them, whilst an intimate friend of mine, Mr. David Waddington, became his vice-chairman, and together they amassed a considerable fortune. Mr. Geo. Hudson came to London, took one of the newly-erected mansions at Albert Gate, and gave a series of splendid dinners and entertainments, presided over by Mrs. Hudson, who, being one of *les nouveaux riches*, was made the shaft of many funny stories, similar to those attributed to the heroic Mrs. Ramsbotham. The Railway King had his levees attended by many of the leaders of both Houses of Parliament; members of the Royal Family were not ashamed to be amongst the numbers who flocked to his house; and the lately-elected member for Sunderland completely carried London society by storm. Then came the dire crash about 1850; every one "went for" George Hudson; a large sum of money, amounting to some £200,000, he was forced to disgorge by order of the Courts. He was obliged to give up his seat in Parliament and to retire to the Continent, where he lived on the wretched remnants of his fortune; till at last, reduced almost to want, a subscription was started for him amongst those who had not only partaken of his boundless hospitality, but had made comparatively large fortunes from his various railway schemes.

I remember I assisted to complete the plans for the Midland Grand Junction, which ran from Northampton to Reading. I shall never forget the night of the 30th November, 1847, which was the last night for depositing the plans. The White Hart at Aylesbury was filled with engineers, lawyers, parliamentary agents, and their satellites, and as each batch of plans was completed and rolled up, the post-chaises rattled out of the yard, from mid-day to nine p.m., and the plans were despatched by them to Oxford, Reading, Hertford, Bedford, and Northampton. It was nearly eight o'clock before the plans for Northampton were ready; an engine with steam up was waiting at the Aylesbury station to take this precious freight to Northampton, nearly fifty miles distant by rail. At length, a couple of clerks carried the documents down to the station and took their seats in a single coach attached to a guard's break and the engine, and off they started. When between Leighton Buzzard and Bletchley, the fuel became exhausted, and the guard and the emissaries jumped down and tore up some of the rails which fenced the line, broke them up, and so kept the fire of the engine going until they arrived at Bletchley, where they replenished, and again started on their journey. This delay caused them more than half an hour's loss of time, and it was a quarter to twelve when they neared Northampton station. On arriving they sprang out of the carriage, and ran off up the steep hill to the office of the Clerk of the Peace in the Market Square, and rapped hurriedly at the door, just before the church clock struck twelve. No one answered their repeated knockings, and a policeman informed them that the Clerk of the Peace had arranged that the plans should be brought to his private house, about five minutes' distance off; but when they arrived there the official refused to receive them, as it was past twelve o'clock at night. They remonstrated with him, and said they could prove their presence at his proper official residence before twelve, and insisted on depositing their plans. During the altercation, the door being open, they threw the plans into the house, and ran back to the station, returned on the engine, and arrived at Aylesbury about three o'clock in the morning. On a full representation of the facts before the Standing Orders Committee, it was decided that the plans were to be deemed in time, as, by the evidence of the policeman, they were at the Clerk's official place for deposit before the hour named. It must have cost the company at least £50 to deposit this one set of plans.

It is impossible to measure the reckless extravagance which was practised at this time in the parliamentary contests of rival lines, and for which, even to the present day, the travelling public are still obliged to pay. This needless outlay was mainly brought about by the orders and regulations of Parliament itself. It was at that time necessary that personal notice should be served on every owner of property, however small, along which the line passed; and as a friend of mine was on the staff of Messrs. Crowdey and Maynard, solicitors to the Eastern Counties Line, he obtained the appointment for me to serve the notices on those owners of property on the Tilbury and Southend Line who resided in Ireland. It was the year of the great famine, and I was anxious to judge for myself the real state of the famine-stricken Irish people.

I received instructions to proceed at once to Dublin, with £50 in bank-notes and gold to pay my expenses, and, further, always "to travel like a gentleman," to hire post-horses, four if necessary—the notices were all to be served by the 5th of December.

In Limerick the evidence of the famine was very apparent; nothing could exceed the misery, starvation, and wretchedness of the people. The relief works were in full operation, chiefly consisting of the breaking up of some of the finest roads in the world, and running them even, under pretence of lowering the hills and filling up the valleys! The Government of the day had defeated a statesman-like proposal of Lord George Bentinck, to lay out several millions on railway works, which would, by this time, have been of inestimable benefit to Ireland. My tour was cut short by a letter from my sisters, asking me to hurry home, as my father was most dangerously ill. I therefore went through to London and reported myself, handing in my account— between four and five pounds left out of the fifty pounds given me for expenses. I was told I need not be so particular in my cash statements, and that I had better keep the balance. I dined with the staff, and was then requested to accompany the cashier into his office, who said, "Let me see, you have been sixteen days on your journey; you are entitled to £2 2s. a day for your services," and he gave me a cheque for £33 12s. I

THE RAILWAY MANIA.

believe the two properties for which I had to serve notices were not worth together more than £150; and I received £83 12s. alone for this work, which can now be done by two penny stamped letters.

In less than a year afterwards the crash came, and most of the great fortunes accumulated during the previous six years crumbled to the dust. Many families were brought to the very verge of ruin by the rampant speculation and inordinate competition to obtain possession of certain districts of the country, in the hope of aiding and swelling the already overgrown businesses of some of the existing great railway companies.

Amongst the most bitter opponents of railways, as a landowner, was the Duke of Buckingham, the father of the late Duke. One of the projected lines, at the time of which I am now writing, went through the Duke's property at Stowe, near Buckingham, and he raised a complete *posse comitatus* of his labourers and dependents to oppose the survey. A raw Irishman, named Oliver Byrne, was the engineer of the line, and numerous affrays took place between his chainmen and assistant surveyors and the Duke's *posse;* there was many a fight and breaking of heads, and every obstacle was raised to prevent a survey being made and the levels taken. Large sheets and tarpaulins were suspended on poles, and stretched across fields and roads in the vain hope of preventing the theodolites being used. At last, one night, Oliver Byrne galloped up to the White Hart in a chaise and four, shouting, "I've done the Duke, I've done the Duke"; and, overjoyed at his success, celebrated his triumph in libations of champagne. It appears he obtained two moderately-sized ladders, and, with a strong body of men, planted them on a footpath which made the base line of his survey, stationing here one surveyor with a theodolite, strongly attached to the rounds of one ladder, and another with a similar arrangement fifty yards off, and by this expedient he succeeded in taking his levels and survey, looking over the obstacles erected by the Duke's men, and so kept on from distance to distance for more than half a mile over the protected property. Survey work was carried out by moonlight by one staff of men, whilst another lot took up a position on other portions of the estate, to divert the attention of the obstructionists from their proceedings. This is one instance of the difficulties which many of our lines of railway had to overcome, caused by the blind opposition of landowners.

In the original plan of a railway from London to Birmingham, laid down by G. Stephenson, almost every landowner along the line, which has since become the New Metropolitan Railway to Aylesbury, opposed it most bitterly—Cox of Hillingdon, Newdigate of Uxbridge, Way of Denham, Hibbert of Chalfont, Drake of Amersham (with a length of nearly forty-five miles), Lord Carrington, and the Smiths of Wendover, and the then Duke of Buckingham, with all the squirearchy who were under his influence. It was this opposition which drove Stephenson to adopt the present line *viâ* Watford, Tring, and Bletchley. Here, again, the opposition of Lords Essex, Clarendon, and others at the first-named place prevented the company going through their properties, and drove them to the other side of Watford, necessitating the viaduct near Bushey, the long Watford tunnel, the heavy Boxmoor embankment, and the deep chalk cuttings at Tring. It is said that compelling the line to go on the present side of Watford caused an excess in the outlay of a quarter of a million of money more than was contemplated in the original estimate. It was not the landowners only who were at fault; even the great town of Northampton refused the railway access to their town, and banished it to Blisworth, four miles away; while the University authorities at Oxford forced the Great Western to go to Didcot, seven miles distant from their ancient city.

The little Aylesbury railway to Cheddington was the first branch which directly opened into the main line. At the dinner to celebrate the opening of the Aylesbury railway, in responding to his health, Robert Stephenson said, " Whatever may occur, you may rely upon it that the London and Birmingham Railway will never forget its 'eldest child,'" a statement that has been amply fulfilled; it never has forgotten to oppress and injure its poor bantling. It was not till the year 1889, nearly fifty years afterwards, that a new station was built at Aylesbury, the wretchedly small and inconvenient station remaining as it was built at first, although the traffic had increased twenty-fold.

Development of traffic!—The old Aylesbury coach "The Despatch" used to leave the town, previously to the opening of the railway, with what was considered a good fair load of four outside and two inside passengers daily.

About six other coaches passed up to London and down during the day, on an average carrying two passengers each. This would make about twenty-four passengers in and out of the town daily except on Sundays, when the coaches did not run. At the present time, the London and North-Western Railway average, in and out, 450, the Great Western 350, and the little despised Aylesbury and Buckingham 200 daily, making in all 1000 passengers who travel from and to the town every day, Sundays included! And we read of further facilities being required! How the goods and the ordinary supply of food used to be carried to us now seems a wonder. About four broad-wheeled waggons, each drawn by eight powerful horses, passed through the town daily, and a few carriers' carts went twice a week to and from London: the branch of the Grand Junction Canal brought most of the heavy traffic, and all the coal. The town in 1837 contained about 4600 inhabitants, now about 10,000. The surrounding villages and districts remain about the same in population as then. With regard to the coal supply, people can scarcely credit the shifts the inhabitants had to endure before the opening of railways. Many thousand tons were stacked in reserve on the extensive coal wharf of the Grand Junction Canal in the month of September to make ready for the winter: if the canal was frozen over, the supply soon became exhausted, the price, ordinarily 30$s.$ per ton, rose to 40$s.$ and even more. The town and neighbourhood before the canal was opened—1812—must in the winter have been in a deplorable condition. I have heard my father say, that in the great frost which lasted thirteen weeks in 1814, they kept up the kitchen fire only, and in the kitchen the family, the guests, and servants all had to assemble, the heat being kept in with cinders and broken glass. At last my grandfather sent a waggon and four horses from his farm at Amersham some twenty-five miles, fifteen miles from Aylesbury, and another ten miles to Uxbridge, and brought back two tons of Newcastle coal—the coal cost £5 at Uxbridge. Of course, until the railway was opened it was impossible to carry on any large factory in the town, as there were no adequate means of transport to or from the place either for the raw material, coal, or machinery.

A curious prophecy, based on an intuitive idea of the powers of science and of steam, was ventured upon by the late eccentric owner of Hartwell House, Dr. Lee, at our opening railway dinner. In his speech he said, amidst the laughter of the company, "I should not be surprised if the day would come when, in addition to our Aylesbury branch, we should see a little branch to Thame, another to Princes Risbro', another to Waddesdon, and another to Wendover; and perhaps some of us may live to see this." The three first have long been in use—and I am glad to say I have, in conjunction with the learned doctor and Sir Harry Verney, had a hand in carrying these through—the last, to Wendover, through the instrumentality of the Metropolitan Company, is now an accomplished fact, and the despised, condemned, and ridiculed Aylesbury and Buckingham Railway will become a portion of a great main line from London to the North of England.

I first became acquainted with the late Duke of

Buckingham and Chandos about the year 1860, in connection with railway business, and our pleasant relations once begun continued to the time of his Grace's lamented death. I had seen and known a great deal of him from his youth upwards, and believe there seldom was a more honourable, trustworthy, hardworking, able man. When the great crash in his father's affairs came, our world held the opinion that the fortune of the family could never again be in the ascendant. It was in the year 1847 that the blow fell which deprived the then Marquis of Chandos of his ancestral home and patrimony. His grandfather, the first Duke of Buckingham, when Marquis of Buckingham, married the daughter, and only child, of the Duke of Chandos, a man of illustrious descent, whose ancestor, knighted on the field of Agincourt as Sir Richard Chandos, became ennobled by successive sovereigns, till the title died out when the family was only represented by this daughter.

Soon after the coronation of George IV. the Marquis of Chandos was created Duke of Buckingham and Chandos, thus reviving the title of his wife's father. Their eldest son, Richard Plantagenet Nugent Bridges Temple Grenville (truly a galaxy of names!), was the well-known Marquis of Chandos, the "Farmers' Friend," and undoubtedly the most popular man amongst the agriculturists in the kingdom. The celebrated "Chandos Clause," moved and carried by him in the House of Commons during the debates on the great Reform Bill of the Whig Government of 1832, enfranchised the £50 renter of land, and this clause was fraught with weighty consequence to the future government of the country, as it imparted a strong Conservative element to the new constitution, and enabled the Tory party a few years afterwards, under Sir Robert Peel, and his active, youthful right hand, the present Mr. W. E. Gladstone, to resume the government. The ruling passion of the Marquis of Chandos, when he succeeded to the dukedom, was territorial aggrandisement and power, and every estate that fell either under the auctioneer's hammer, or was sold by private contract in Bucks, was swallowed by his capacious maw; old mansions were either razed to the ground or turned into farmhouses—in many instances they were suffered to fall into decay—that he might be really lord paramount, and that so far as political power was concerned nothing should "stand between the wind and his nobility." Money was borrowed at 5 per cent. or more, to pay for properties that would scarcely yield 2 per cent., as he paid most exorbitant prices for land; and, to pose as the farmers' friend and to gain political power, he let his farms at absurdly low rents. To this must be added considerable sums spent in elections and expensive establishments at Wotton and Stowe: it was only a question of time, therefore, how long this would continue.

The whole matter culminated in a grand celebration of the coming of age of his only son, the late Duke. Her Majesty the Queen and Prince Albert graced Stowe with their presence to do honour to the descendant of the younger royal line of the Plantagenets, the Duke being descended from Mary, the widow of Louis, King of France, the younger sister of Henry

VIII., who was afterwards married to Charles Brandon, Duke of Suffolk. The magnificence with which this royal visit was carried out almost exceeds belief. A great part of Stowe was newly furnished, and the state bedroom was a marvel of expensive upholstery. All the county assembled there; the tenants were fêted, the tradesmen, their families and friends, of the borough of Buckingham and Aylesbury were right royally entertained; balls, concerts, and yeomanry fêtes were the order of the day. These festivities continued for the greater part of a week, and the London and local papers utilized all their stock of adjectives in describing the splendour of the entertainment. I have been told that the young Marquis, even while the Queen and Prince were being entertained, was taken into the library and, in utter ignorance of their import, signed papers which practically alienated the greater part of the landed property, and left him comparatively a beggar. In less than two years after this the sheriff was in possession of Stowe, and the whole of the magnificent furniture, gems of art, statuary, and pictures, collected at enormous cost in Italy and elsewhere by the first Duke, was brought to the hammer. The sale lasted twenty-eight days. Never was such a complete destruction of a great property before in England. The Duke and Duchess, with their son the Marquis of Chandos, were left absolutely without a furnished home.

I have given this sketch of a ruined house to illustrate the difficulties the late Duke had to contend with from the outset of his career. The Norwich Union and some other great insurance offices had heavy policies on the life of the Duke, and knowing the perfect integrity and business-like habits of the Marquis of Chandos, they made him manager or steward of the Wotton estate, giving him, I am told, £1500 per annum as a salary, out of which, in a most disinterested way, he gave his father £500 a year to enable him to live in comfort at the Great Western Hotel at Paddington, and to his mother the Duchess the same, she having been lent by the Queen a suite of apartments at Hampton Court. Wotton had been partly refurnished, and the Marquis resided there, superintended the labourers on the estate, looked after the land drainage, cutting off water-courses, felling and sawing up timber, and all the various operations of land management. I have many times seen him, whilst I was hunting with the Bicester hounds, standing up to his ankles in clay laying out and planning water-courses and drains, and thoroughly looking after upwards of a hundred labourers. After a year or two he married a very amiable lady, Miss Harvey of Langley Park, to whom he was greatly attached, and who bore him three daughters. With her, I heard, he had about £1000 a year from her father; and his mechanical and business-like habits, his love of railway work and knowledge of locomotive engines, earned him the position of Chairman of the London and North-Western Railway, with a salary of £2500 per annum.

The Marquis from that time, with his very modest requirements, was able to save money. The Duke, his father, somewhat suddenly died; the life policies for which his life was insured fell in, and I believe something like £170,000 became payable, and with this the new Duke entirely freed the Wotton estate, and with the surplus was enabled to purchase back in a few years some of the outlying farms. The death also of his mother, which grieved him greatly, as he was deeply attached to her, was followed, in about three years, by that of her brother the Marquis of Breadalbane, who, having no lineal descendants, left his nephew the Duke nearly a quarter of a million cash! Here was then a climax, and a *solatium* for his hard-earned and laborious exertions to maintain his honour and family fame untarnished.

The Duke lost the position, however, of Chairman of the London and North-Western Railway, through the Liverpool and Manchester school thinking that he looked too much after minor details and failed to grasp more extended fields of operation afforded by the large manufacturing districts of the North of England. Whatever may have been their ideas, I think it redounds greatly to his credit that he foresaw the necessity of doubling the line of railway, and it was during his reign that the third line of railway was laid down, which has now culminated in four lines reaching to Rugby. When the Duke first insisted upon the laying down of a third line, one of the leading engineers sneered at the idea: " like the fifth wheel to a coach," he said it would be.

A gentleman with whom I had some connection in railway matters a few years before, called on me one day in 1860 with Mr. Brydone, who was at that time engineer to the Great Northern Railway, and wished to consult me respecting a proposed line to Thame. I told them it was useless to go there, as a bill had been obtained in Parliament by the Great Western branch to run from Maidenhead to High Wycombe, and from thence to Oxford; but if they would be guided by me I would show them a projected portion of old George Stephenson's original line from London to Birmingham, which was afterwards partly carried out by his son Robert, but which had never been completed between Claydon and Aylesbury. I took them over my suggested route through Quainton to Claydon so as to join the Buckinghamshire line, which ran from Bletchley to Banbury and Oxford. The Marquis of Chandos was then Chairman of the London and North-Western Railway, and on our return we determined to consult his lordship, and called at Wotton. Fortunately we found him at home, and he fell in with our views immediately; said he would become chairman of our company, and would take £5000 in shares if we brought it out. When our surveys were made, the bill deposited in Parliament, and the company formed, he carried out his promises, became our chairman, and launched the project. Through his indefatigable zeal and business-like ability the line, after many years of trouble and disaster, was completed and opened. I joined the Board of Directors at the commencement, and Sir Harry Verney became vice-chairman with a representative board of directors—Sir Harry and myself are the only men of the original Board now alive.

We directors had reason to congratulate ourselves upon the Duke of Buckingham's acuteness and remarkable knowledge of minor details as to business management. The secretary to the company, shortly after the line was opened, reported to the Board that, as there were several level crossings chiefly of an occupation nature, he had thought it necessary to have some special padlocks made for the gates, in order to prevent people from opening them, and leaving them open, to the danger of the traffic on the line. He showed us the keys, which were very elaborate with complicated wards, to cost 5s. 6d. each, a charge which his Grace thought excessive. He left the Board-room with a key in his hand unknown to us, and sent one of the clerks for a piece of soap. He then quietly pressed the soap into the wards of the key and put it into the lock, and on withdrawing the key showed it to us with the soap intact in the wards, a proof that the whole apparent intricacy was a Brummagem fraud, that there were no obstructions whatever in the locks, and that any key, or even an old bent nail, would open them. The value of the locks was about 10d. or 1s. each, but neither the secretary nor any of those present would ever have thought of such a test.

I have been told that the Duke constantly, when Chairman of the London and North-Western Railway, drove the engine from London for very long distances, carefully noting every hundredweight of fuel consumed, the quantity of oil for engines, and comparing it with the speed at which the engine travelled, and that he even noted the quantity of cotton-waste consumed on the journey. He had a keen eye for every detail of any business with which he was connected. But besides being an able business man, he was a just and a generous one. When the rinderpest broke out in the county the Duke was indefatigable in carrying out the regulations of the Government as to slaughter of the infected cattle, but he shared all the losses of this dire scourge with his tenants. Again, whilst himself in the East, as Governor of Madras, there had been on his Wotton estate a terrible outbreak of liver rot, which carried off every sheep in the parish except ten or twelve Welsh ewes; the Duke ordered his steward to ascertain how much loss each of his tenants had sustained, and on the next rent-day each tenant had the full amount of his loss deducted from his rent, and in most instances the tenants left the steward's office with some scores of pounds more than when they went in. One man told me that above a £100 had been handed to him beyond his half-year's rent. These were noble and disinterested acts, most unostentatiously done, and springing from a kind and considerate heart. In person and manners the Duke was not attractive, but he possessed qualities more valuable than those reflected in the glass of fashion; his death was not only a grief to his friends, but a loss to the nation, whom he had served as a Minister of the Crown. He had raised himself from real poverty by his assiduity and careful personal management, he had succeeded in freeing his estate from encumbrances, refurnished Stowe, buying back, wherever he could find them, everything that had been sold at the great sale, and he left behind him something like £120,000 for his daughters and their husbands.

The family estate of Wotton went at his death to his nephew, Mr. Gore Langton, heir to the title of Earl Temple; his eldest daughter, Lady Mary, the wife of

Captain Morgan, became possessed of Stowe, and succeeded to the title of Baroness Kinloss. The dukedom, in default of male heirs, became extinct for the fourth or fifth time. It is remarkable that there have been so many Dukes of Buckingham, in so many different families, which have in turn died out for want of heirs male: the celebrated Duke in the time of Richard III., the Staffords, the Villiers in the time of Charles, and now the Grenvilles—it would seem that a fatality attached to this great and historic title.

Another excellent specimen of the old country gentleman was Sir Thomas Aubrey. He was Chairman of the Quarter Sessions for many years; he wore generally a blue coat, gilt buttons, a buff waistcoat, and large shirt frill projecting from the front. Many a quaint story is told of him when on the bench. A man was once tried before him for stealing ducks, and the jury found him "Not guilty." Sir Thomas then addressed him and said: "Prisoner at the bar, you have had a very narrow escape, and when you go next over Priestwood Common, *don't you steal ducks again.*" Once a witness came up to give a man under trial a character; the prisoner was quite unknown to the Bench, and the witness on being asked what he knew of the prisoner gave the usual stereotyped answer, "He never knowed nothing amiss of him before then." Sir Thomas said, "Nor more did I; if that's all you have to say about him you may sit down." Sir Thomas, when Colonel Aubrey, once started as a candidate for the Borough of Aylesbury, but did not venture to go to the poll. He was nephew to Sir John Aubrey, of Dorton, who, when he died, left all the family estates he possibly could away from his nephew, as Sir Thomas had married a young lady contrary to his wishes. She died within a year or so of her marriage, childless. Sir Thomas never married again, and as Sir John had left the estates to a stranger, and had leased the Welsh and other properties at very long leases and at ridiculously low rates, so as to impoverish his nephew as much as possible, it may be imagined that Sir Thomas did not trouble himself to improve the estates. I once visited his ancient mansion and park, Llantrithet, near Cardiff, with his steward, and found the deer destroyed, the house nearly dismantled, and the estate almost denuded of timber.

This Sir John Aubrey was for some years member for the County of Bucks, and stood the celebrated poll for the election in 1784, when he was returned at the head of the poll over the Hon. Thomas Grenville and Lord Verney. One amusing record we have of that election. Sir John knew there were many residents in the borough and county who were above receiving ordinary money bribes, so he was accustomed to invite a rather aristocratic party to dine at Dorton House, and by the side of each guest on the dinner-table was placed a handsome silver cup, which at the conclusion of the entertainment each gentleman was expected to put into his pocket and carry home with him as a memento of his visit. On the cup was inscribed, " May voters be free, and representatives independent." I have seen many of these cups, which are now becoming very rare; the late Mr. James bought several, and I believe some are in the collections of the Rothschild family.

CHAPTER XI.

University Steeplechase Meeting at Banbury—A Nasty Brook—A Famous Race over the Broughton Farm—A Horse comes Upstairs—Leech Manning rides the little Grey Mare over the Dining-room Table Gambling and Betting—A Captain who pursued Welshers—Of a Fool and his Folly - A Salt-water Tragedy.

IN the year 1848 or 1849 I was at Banbury attending the Oxford University Steeplechases, and in the evening, after the sport had concluded for the day, an objection was made to a horse that had run on the wrong side of a flag. Angry words were used, and the dispute grew fast and furious, when at last it was agreed to refer the matter to the late Mr. Henry Cooper, a well-known sporting draper in Banbury, who, after hearing the dispute, gave his decision, the purport however of which I forget. So exasperating was it to the losing party, chiefly consisting of undergraduates, that they vowed they would never go to Banbury again, and asked me if I would allow them to use the Aylesbury course, which was at that time over my father's farm at Broughton, near Aylesbury. I at once consented, and the next year they came to the old town; but as there had been a race over a very severe course on the other side of the town a few weeks before, the undergraduates determined to hold their first meeting there. This course started near the County Infirmary grounds, and after passing over three or four grass fields the line crossed the Bicester turnpike road; after two more grass enclosures came "The Brook," a rattling good one, about sixteen feet wide, no fence on the take-off side, but fair naked water; the line then ran over a very strong country, with stiffest of "bullfinchers," as far as Dr. Lee's park at Hartwell.

The race—over seventeen riders came to the post—was won by the well-known gentleman jock, familiarly called Jemmy Allgood, of Brasenose College, and much liked in University circles, on a mare belonging to Charlie Symonds, named Freshwater; the second was Kathleen, ridden by Mr. Bunney; and then came one of my old friend Joe Tollitt's string, his well-seasoned horse Valiant. Joe Tollitt still lives, an octogenarian, or very near it, and is young-looking and as hearty as ever, thanks to the glorious old vintage port which he has always patronized, and which he still thoroughly enjoys, but, I must do him the justice to add, always in moderation.

At this meeting an amusing incident occurred which may be worth chronicling. A match was ridden between A. W. Myers, on a mare called Clementina, and a horse called Sailor. Myers, on coming near the dreaded brook, fairly funked, and in the middle of the grass field threw himself off his mount and left his mare to herself. An undergraduate named Mr. Burlton in a most plucky manner rushed forward, caught the mare's bridle, vaulted into the vacant saddle, sent her at a rattling pace at the brook, and clearing the water-jump in splendid style, rode the whole course, challenged the Sailor when nearing home, when both horses raced at a clipping pace at the brook again on the return journey, and both cleared it, but the amateur was first to pass the winning-post. Although Burlton pulled the scales down, the decision was given however against his winning the race, and the Sailor was declared the winner.

It was after this meeting, in the next year, that arrangements were made to run over the Broughton country. This had been made famous as the line over which the celebrated race was run in which the four leading steeplechasers of the day put to the test their skill as fencers, and their mettle as racers. This wonderful, perhaps matchless quartet, consisted of Mr. Vevers' Vainhope, four years old, 9st. 10lbs., ridden by William Archer, the father of the noted and still lamented "Freddy Archer"; Mr. Elmore's British Yeoman, aged, 11st., ridden by Jem Mason; Mr. Clark's Maria Day, ridden by Frisbey, 10st. 5lbs., aged; and Mr. Hassell's The Young 'Un, five years old, 10st. 2lbs., ridden by Tom Ablett. Five others started, all of public or local celebrity, and an immense concourse of spectators assembled on Broughton Farm to see these animals try their best over a course such as had never been crossed before. Starting in a meadow adjoining the arm of the Grand Junction Canal to Aylesbury, they crossed three large grass fields to a mill-stream, the take-off being on a rising ground and an ugly descent for the landing; across the turnpike road out of which an awkward double had to be negotiated, over steep ridge and furrow grass meadows into four fields of heavy plough; then, turning to the left near to the village of

Weston Turville, the line came to a small brook with a stiff eight feet high "bullfincher," uncut—as every fence was that day; bearing to the left again, they recrossed the turnpike, skirted the Tring road over four grass fields, crossed the winning-field, and, turning round a flag to the right, the mill-dam had to be jumped a second time; then over three more great grass enclosures, with rattling "bullfinchers" and one smart double; and then a straight half-mile home, over a big stake and binder newly laid down, to the mill-dam, with its rising take-off and a deep drop on landing, into a small grass field, and, to get out of it, they had to jump a tremendous single, with a broad ditch on the landing side, into the winning-field: the run in was about four hundred yards up a steep incline. Here assembled the crowd of both sexes, and, as the horses could be seen for more than half a mile to the finish, the excitement was well sustained.

When the brook was jumped, all four were together, Vainhope and British Yeoman being a few lengths in advance of Maria Day and the Young 'Un. The two former came along breasting the last fence together; each making an enormous jump they landed safely, and such a set-to has seldom been seen as between the accomplished riders Jem Mason and W. Archer; but the extra weight on the Yeoman told in the end, and Vainhope came in the winner by a length, the third and fourth being only a few lengths behind. All the horses were pumped out; the winner only four years old! Mr. Elmore, the owner of the Yeoman, was dreadfully disappointed—he had made sure of the success of his party, the well-known stamina of his horse, and the fact of his being steered by the "Prince of Steeplechase Riders," giving them every confidence. Mr. Vevers, the owner of Vainhope, was also pretty sure of victory, as in addition to his horse's brilliant fencing he had an extraordinary turn of speed, and his trainer, Bradshaw, was equally confident, if only the horse could be kept on his legs. About a mile from the finish, I was standing with Bradshaw, and as Vainhope passed he was lying second and going strong and well, but throwing his head about and sprinkling his sides and neck with white foam. I said, "The horse seems beaten." Bradshaw answered, "That's just what I want him to look; so long as he can do that he's all right. He is a very free sweater, and in tip-top condition, and so long as he can perspire freely he can never be beaten." The result proved how true this opinion was.

The race took over twenty-two minutes to run; and as some doubt was expressed as to the distance, the riders saying they were sure it was over four miles, Messrs. Hall and Baker, who in conjunction with myself had laid out the course, measured it then and there, when we found it to have been over five miles and a half. It was therefore in length almost unprecedented; the fences were in a perfectly natural state, uncut, and only marked here and there with a single flag: never before or since has such a race been run, for after this time more care has been taken to measure the course correctly.

It should be mentioned, as a remarkable circumstance, and as an instance of what a really good steeplechaser of unequalled stamina and power can do, that in jumping the last fence into the winning-field, every one present was astonished at the apparent space the horses cleared; and soon after the race was over, the distance from where their fore-feet left the ground to the points where their hind-feet indented the turf was measured, and it was found that a space of thirty-four feet seven inches had been cleared—this too after running five miles and three chains over the stiff and varied course I have endeavoured to describe.

In the year 1851, at one of the early meetings of the Aylesbury Aristocratic Steeplechases, and during the stewards' dinner at the White Hart in the grand old Rochester Room, the following event occurred.

The conversation turned to the fact that the Marquis of Waterford had once taken a noted hunter up the stairs and led him round the dining-table in this very room, whilst the noble Master of the Buckhounds, the Earl of Erroll, and his guests fed the horse on biscuits and apples—the Marquis afterwards leading him downstairs again into the entrance hall. One of the young Oxford gentlemen, well known for his splendid riding in the steeplechases which were then being held, turned to old Charlie Symonds and said, " I believe, Charlie, the little grey would come up these or any other stairs." It was asked if the trial might be made, and, on consent being obtained, down went two or three choice spirits into the stable-yard, and, to the astonishment of the party (nearly fifty people being present), a lumbering noise was heard on the stairs, and presently in walked the gallant grey. After leading him round the table and resting him before a large fire which blazed in the fine old grate before which many a time and oft poor Nellie Gwynne had warmed her dainty feet, the horse, led by a halter, was induced to jump over the backs of a couple of chairs. Then, J. Leech Manning, a sporting farmer of the neighbourhood, said he would undertake to ride him over the dinner-table (it should be mentioned that the dinner was still in progress, the third course was being consumed, the decanters of wine going their round, the candelabra all alight, and various wax lights as well were sparkling on the board). No sooner said than Manning jumped on to the barebacked horse, and taking the halter in his hand, he rode him up into the corner of the room, which was about forty feet long by twenty-two feet wide, the table in the meantime having been slightly slued round : Manning struck the horse with his heel, and with a slap on his neck with his right hand he sent him flying over the table, covered as it was with all the usual appurtenances to a repast: he cleared it well, then, to the surprise of all, he turned the horse in splendid style and jumped him back again.

The gentleman who first suggested the attempt, now a noted parish priest in an extreme northern county, then essayed the same feat. The horse answered to his cry of "Come up," and just cleared the table, but caught one of his heels on its edge, and pulling the cloth over smashed a few plates and glasses, which fell with a loud clatter, whereupon the rider struck the gallant steed with his open hand, and again he cleared the whole in much better style than before. Of course, immediately a dozen others, emulous

THE JUMP OVER THE DINNER-TABLE.

To face page 174.

of fame, wished to essay the feat, but I thought there had been enough done to try the temper of the noble little horse, and a veto was put on any more displays of circus riding. Then the difficulty arose—How are we to get the horse to descend the stairs ? From the Rochester Room to the top of the staircase there was a long gallery with floor of polished oak, and this gallery had to be traversed before the descent commenced ; a narrow carpet ran the entire length, and along this the horse went quietly enough, but on coming to the top of the stairs he stoutly refused to make the descent. Nothing we could do would induce him to put his foot downwards on to the first step, and although all the time he was as quiet as a lamb, no one could suggest a means of overcoming his scruples at taking so unusual a course. In this dilemma a learned Q.C., who was staying in the house, who had started as candidate to represent the ancient borough of Aylesbury in Parliament, and, with him, his elder brother, a worthy baronet and M.P. for a county borough, hearing the noise on the stairs came from their sitting-room, and at once suggested an easy solution of the difficulty, viz. to tie a wet towel over the horse's head, blindfold him, take him to the end of the long corridor, and then to lead him steadily along without stopping a moment, but to keep him going without any hesitation. This advice was no sooner given than it was put into practice, and the horse coming along freely enough, he began to go down the stairs, but getting frightened he stumbled and fell on his knees, but did not cease to scramble on. The two men who held him tightly by the head evidently reassured the well-trained dining-room performer, and in the end he landed safely in the entrance hall, merely breaking three or four of the carved oak balusters.

This stands out an unique feat of horsemanship, for it must be remembered that when the Marquis of Waterford, assisted by Mr. Ricardo, brought his horse into the room they did not attempt any riding. At the time the grey accomplished its feat, a youthful earl, then an undergraduate at Oxford, was in the chair at the dinner, who is now a noble duke, renowned for his thorough devotion to the duties of his station, and well known by every one in the "land o' cakes." Some year or so after, the talented horse was bought by a worthy Quaker at Leighton Buzzard, and a noted judge of horseflesh, who was always pleased to show his friends the gallant grey that had jumped the table in the Rochester Room at Aylesbury.

Whenever I had the opportunity I endeavoured to keep down betting and gambling during the 'Varsity Steeplechases, and can boast of having been more or less successful. The gambling done by and between themselves as members of the 'Varsity was not a serious matter, as their own money passed backwards and forwards between them, and in the end not much harm was done; but when strangers and adventurers came down, hoping to rob the undergraduates with impunity, I was determined to do my very best to get rid of them. Ordinarily the wagers between undergraduates took the form of backing their own mounts, or one old University favourite against another; but sometimes they extended into occasional hazards on the great public races, and, as the 'Varsity meetings were held generally in March, the Derby and Oaks were, at times, somewhat heavily speculated upon: I myself was never a man to bet more than a few pounds on the big races. At one of these University meetings, after dinner, I was asked my opinion of the next year's Derby; I said I had a fancy for West-Australian. I was told he had no chance, and a Mr.—well! I will leave his name a blank—offered me £50 to £4, which I took, and another, who was only a visitor, a Captain K——, said that I had laid my money out badly, and he would give me 15 to 1, £60 to £4, against him. This being very tempting, contrary to my usual custom I took it, thus standing to win £110 or lose £8. The horse rose rapidly in the betting, and about six weeks afterwards, knowing that a wager was not "well made till it was well hedged," I laid a certain sporting parson or "Squarson" £40 to £8 against the horse, thus standing to win £70 and lose nothing. To my delight West-Australian won. On the following market-day, when my clerical friend appeared, I joyfully gave him my cheque for £40. I regret to say I never received one farthing of my £110.

My disgust was so great, that I resolved never again to bet on a horse-race. The former young gentleman, then of Merton College, came to a regular smash; the last I heard of Captain K—— was, that about three years afterwards he took a very prominent part in heading a party at the Doncaster St. Leger who were pursuing a "Welsher," whom they stripped of his clothes, and, I believe, soundly thrashed; the scamp in truth being quite as deserving of that treatment himself, if we are to judge the indignant captain by the way he had behaved to me and to others.

As to gambling, "the Boys" played Van John, and fairly won of each other many a fiver perhaps, but knowing that I discountenanced anything like a regular gambling-table, they never ventured to introduce those worthies who make it a practice to fleece all with whom they come in contact. On one occasion, however, after the banquet on the first day of the meeting, the entries for the "Open Handicap" were handed in, and I myself and two competent assistants were selected as handicappers, and went up-stairs to a private room to complete our work. On opening the door a well-dressed man in bland terms begged of us to come in and join the party. The room was already occupied, and our indignation was aroused by seeing a regular table set out for play, and, at the head of it, some well-known "hell-keepers" from London. The table was surrounded by a choice party of the guests who had been dining with us, prominent among them a duke and viscount. The champagne was flowing freely, the party much excited and in full play at rouge et noir or roulette, baccarat being then unknown. I told them at once that if they did not immediately break up the table and disperse, I would fetch the police and have them all taken into custody; and I threatened the proprietor of the hotel that I would have him and his house indicted if the gambling was not instantly put a stop to. The duke and his friends begged of me and my brother handicappers to withdraw, and promised they would stop the play; but we on our side were inexorable and stayed in the room until the table was removed, and the party dispersed. The proprietors of the table, not having been more than two hours at play, had won over £1,400, the duke having contributed £800, and the unhappy viscount £300. The oddity of the story lay in the fact that the duke himself had brought these rascals and their play appliances down with him.

There are worse dangers, however, than the fascination of gambling, and worse disasters than any loss of money. My third brother, who had commenced his seafaring career as a midshipman in the service of the old East India Company, used to tell a tale of a tragedy, the chief scenes of which took place upon a vessel of which he was chief officer, though only twenty-five years of age. It was a fine vessel, one of Mr. Green's, bound to Sydney *viâ* the Cape, and then for Madras. The commander was a popular young officer, who in a previous voyage had become enamoured of a fascinating young widow, who had a child of about six years old, and had married her. In less than a month from his marriage he took this new command. I went on the vessel from Blackwall to Plymouth to see the last of my brother. At Plymouth the captain joined the ship with his wife, but there was not sufficient accommodation on board for the nurse and child. The lady indignantly refused to make the journey without her child, and the result was that the ship sailed with the captain, while his wife and her child remained behind.

The captain was a handsome and gentleman-like fellow, and an experienced seaman. Amongst the passengers was a captain of the English army, who had with him his wife and family of young children, the youngest a baby in arms. All went pleasantly enough on the voyage to the Cape, though my brother observed that his commander paid marked attention to the army captain's wife, who was a very handsome woman. On their arrival at Port Stephens, the military captain disembarked and took up his residence there, and the naval captain was an admitted visitor to his house, and became a too frequent attendant on the lady of the household. The ship remained about a fortnight loading her cargo, and then one fine night weighed anchor and sailed for Madras. On my brother taking charge of the watch at four o'clock a.m., one of the seamen told him that a boat with the commander in it had come alongside soon after twelve o'clock, and that he was accompanied by the captain's wife, and that she was aboard. My brother was indignant, and immediately went to the commander's cabin, and asked if the story were true. "Yes," he said; "her husband has behaved ill to her, and she has determined to go home to her friends. She has placed herself under my protection, and I have consented to take her on to Madras, and send her home overland to England." My brother was determined to be no party to the proceedings, and declared that he would "put the ship about" and land the lady at Port Stephens. The captain then asserted his authority, and forbade his doing so, and he, as chief officer, knew he was powerless, but determined when the vessel got to her destination to send a full account of the proceeding to Messrs. Green, and exonerate himself and his brother officers from all responsibility in the transaction.

On arriving at Madras the lady went ashore with the captain, and for nearly six weeks the captain rarely visited the ship; but she again took up her quarters when the ship set sail to the Mauritius. The night before the vessel set off again for England, the captain sent for my brother, who found him in his cabin, with his head buried in his hands, sobbing deeply. He told my brother that he was an utterly ruined man; that he was so fascinated by this woman he had given up everything for her; that he dare not face his wife on his return to England, nor the lady's husband; that he knew he was a villain, but was powerless to throw off his infatuation: he therefore had determined to resign his position as captain of the vessel, and to give the command over to my brother, to whom he handed a document recounting all the circumstances, and a statement of accounts, to be delivered to Messrs. Green on arrival in London. In the morning he and the lady who was the cause of his ruin left the ship with all their luggage, and the ship passed into the hands of my brother.

But the tragedy had only begun. The commander's wife was so horrified at the transaction that she lost her senses, and ended her days in an asylum; his father, a well-beloved and earnest parish priest, soon died, broken-hearted at the conduct of his only son. The injured captain sought the relief, and obtained it, of the Divorce Court. What a plot for a novel! but what a pitiful reality! The guilty lovers departed from the Mauritius after some weeks to California, and there he blew his brains out with a pistol, while she took to inordinate drinking, and after the death of her lover became a miserable outcast, and died, so I heard, in the wretchedest poverty.

There are other infatuations than for cards and dice!

CHAPTER XII.

Fox-Hunting and Stag-Hunting—A fine Run with "the Baron"—Lord Lonsdale's Harriers and the Cumberland Bagmen—The Ballad of "The Captive Fox"—Jack Hannan v. Johnny Broome—Men of Peace and War—An Innocent Child, and a Clever Clearance.

IN all the sports of the field that I have indulged in, nothing has given me greater pleasure than being mounted on a good horse, following a gallant pack of hounds over a grass country. More than sixty years of my life having been passed in the midst of the glorious Vale of Aylesbury, I have had opportunities of enjoying this "sport of kings" to the best advantage. I have no intention of writing a homily on hunting, but I cannot resist jotting down a few impressions as they have often struck me.

It has been the custom for many years, and in many counties, to look with contempt on stag-hunting, and every absurd epithet has been used to prejudice sportsmen against its pursuit. "Calf-hunting" has been the most popular of the cries against it; but why "calf"? There are many and good reasons for the popularity of stag-hunting in certain favoured districts. I am an old fox-hunter, and an ardent admirer of the pursuit of

"Reynard," and freely admit that no pleasure is so great as a meet on a fine day at the covert-side. There with a cheery word for all, is the gallant master, a country gentleman living on his own estate, dispensing the hospitality of the district, his house the rendezvous of all true sportsmen; the squire's lady and the family beloved by the villagers, and ingratiating themselves with the residents in the district. There, representatives of the peerage and other sporting gentry have plenty to say to the farmers and riding tradesmen of the nearest towns; mutual admiration of each other's horses and opinions as to their merits freely pass, and a recounting of noted runs in which either played a prominent part forms a plentiful source of conversation. At length the hounds are put into cover, till first a whimper, then a challenge from an old hound, and the stentorian cry of the huntsman, with "Tally-ho! Gone away!" echoes through the wood, a rattling run of fifty minutes, the fox pulled down fairly in the open, and every one who had a chance of getting away and maintaining his place good, exults in the success of the day: probably another covert is drawn, and another fox found, is either lost or is run to ground; and then men quietly jog home, highly gratified with their day's sport. Well, that is a pleasant picture; but now look at the reverse one, and it is no exaggeration to say it is of constant occurrence, even in the best of countries. Instead of a fine cheery morning, a raw cold mist; a ride about the covert-side in a deep clay district, while the thick haze turns to a cold drizzle. The hounds draw blank! What is to be done now? Another covert is two miles off; on you jog, turn the collar of your coat up, scarcely exchange a word with your neighbours; at last, in a pelting shower, the hounds are put into the gorse, and again—*blank!* Nothing daunted, on you trot again. It gets late in the afternoon; the hounds feather out of covert without even a whimper: a few minutes' conversation, and then the hounds, with heads and sterns down, drag along the road a miserable ten miles home. You who had ridden ten miles to the meet in the morning, are now fifteen miles from home; about 6.30 you get back; jaded, damp, and tired, you slide off your fagged horse, thoroughly annoyed at a wasted day.

To the man who is fond of hunting, or even may require strong horse exercise for his health, if he lives in the country and amongst a sporting fraternity with whom he can heartily associate, a blank day is not of much consequence; but to the man who lives in London, or in one of the great manufacturing towns, it is of great importance that he should rarely, if ever, be indulged with a luxury of this description. The establishment of so well found and equipped a pack of stag-hounds as those of Lord Rothschild is a real blessing to the urban sportsman—and there are many as true and keen followers of sport in the Metropolis as in the best of the Shires. Men who have their duties to attend to in Parliament or in public offices, others with financial business in the City, and not seldom men engaged in trade, find it of the utmost consequence that they should be spared the annoyance and disappointment of a blank day. To me, it is a pleasant sight to go to Euston station when "The Rothschild" hounds meet in the Vale, or to Paddington when "The Queen's" meet near Slough, and view the crowd of well-dressed men and women who throng the platform, ready to enjoy what they know will be certain sport when they reach the meet; not always, of course, great runs, but never a blank day. Like other packs of hounds, they may have bad scenting days, or the deer may get on to a turnpike road or railway, and run a mile or so on it. But I have seen as grand a run with the stag over a wild country as I ever have with a fox; and of one of such runs—the best run I ever saw in my life—I cannot resist from giving some account.

I rode one bright morning on my not altogether unknown Belzoni mare, as fine a hunter as a man ever could desire, to the meet of "the Baron" at Cublington, about eight miles from Aylesbury. The deer was uncarted and the hounds laid on about 12.30. Not a second did the deer hesitate, but went straight over all the fine grass fields by Aston Abbotts, to the right over the Creslow brook into the noted "Creslow great ground," a magnificent grass enclosure of nearly 400 acres. The brook left at least five-sixths of the field behind, who mostly however overtook the hounds near Whitchurch. "The quarry" then went at a great pace by North Marston and Grandborough over a branch of the Ouse, leaving Winslow to the right, and on to Claydon Woods. Here the hounds were stopped for five minutes, as we had then ridden about twelve miles; and many of the field left, having had their say. On again went the

STAG-HUNTING.

gallant stag over a wild deep country by Marsh Gibbon, tiring the horses sadly, till even that determined sportsman, the late Hon. Robert Grinston, gave up and retired, leaving about a dozen still following. On nearing Launton, about two miles from Bicester, the pack had distanced me, but I kept on their track, and, when Cheslyn Hall came up, we heard some hounds not very far off. We galloped on ; a labourer told us they hadn't been gone above five minutes, and showed us the line they took. After riding nearly a mile we arrived near enough to discover that it was Mr. Drake's hounds we were pursuing, and they were full-cry after a rattling good fox, while the " Staggers," with only five men with them, had gone towards Bucknell. On we pushed our tired steeds, and were soon rewarded by meeting the stag, with three and a half couple of tired hounds following him. The faint music of the hounds infused new life into our horses, and we sped on to the town of Bicester: in a few minutes up came Tom Ball, the huntsman, and two light weights, who always went well—Messrs. T. W. Morris and B. Hawes, then M.P. for Lambeth—and then came one or two stragglers with the rest of the pack. The deer took over a low wall, and went through the gardens at the back of the houses in the main street of the town : I well remember, as I rode down the street, passing that prince of whips, old Sir Henry Peyton, with his four greys and bright yellow coach, and Lady Peyton by his side. The stag took the open again after going through Bicester, and was safely secured about a mile further on, at Langford Farm, the birthplace of Sir Joseph Paxton of Crystal

Palace fame. The inner man was refreshed, and gruel given to our gallant steeds; and, after resting half an hour, I trotted off along the turnpike road, sixteen miles to Aylesbury; the hounds took a cross country route to Mentmore, and, like myself, reached home about 7.30, having ridden at least fifty miles.

The only other class of hunting worthy of record beside fox-hunting and the stag, is that with harriers. It is a charming sight to see a pack of these little "currant jelly" dogs, feathering away under a hedge-row, hunting their hare on her exact track, and filling the air with their lovely music—for no hounds have such music, and give tongue like harriers. I have enjoyed good sport with the late Sir Robert Harvey's and Mr. Harding Cox's harriers; but for the real essence of good sport with harriers the late Lord Lonsdale's was the pack to follow.

The late Earl of Lonsdale kept a pack of harriers at the Harcourt Arms Hotel, by the Tring Station on the London and North-Western Railway, about thirty miles from town. The hounds were drafted from Mr. Drake's and the Old Berkeley foxhounds, and a few from Baron Rothschild's staghounds; and these, with some large-framed harriers, made a rare combination of speedy dogs, and afforded capital sport on the off-days of the stag and foxhound meets. After a time his lordship experienced a great scarcity of hares in the Vale, and he was advised to bring down from his Cumberland estates some wild foxes, and try what he could do with them, on those days when no hare could be found. The "bag foxes," though they afforded excellent sport, were considered Cockney game, beneath the dignity of the real fox-hunter, and great fun was made of their doings. But the Earl was not to be beat, and he determined to see what he could do by hunting and training these Cumberland animals. The Station Hotel was kept by a rare old sportsman, Mr. Sam Brown, a twin-brother of John Brown, who rode his horse Confidence in the first Aylesbury Steeplechase in 1835 (these two men were born in or about 1794, and only joined the majority two or three years since, at ninety-two and ninety-four years of age, and they rode young horses up to three or four years of their decease). There was a large barn adjoining the hotel, and inside it were arranged rows of cages, which contained the foxes; and within the building fences and rails were put up, and their keeper, "the man with the broom," was accustomed every morning to stir up "Reynard," and exercise him backwards and forwards over these artificial fences. On certain days, the Earl and the field would go out and look for a hare, when a man would come up and say, "My Lud, I seed a fox go away yonder." "Thank you, my man," the Earl would reply, giving him half-a-crown; "show me where." Mr. William Reid, who lived at The Node, near Hitchin, and who hunted with the Hertfordshire, was so jealous of the sport these foxes gave that he composed some verses, which were inserted in *Bell's Life*, the then great sporting paper of the day; these were quoted and sung in almost every sporting county in England at that time.

THE CAPTIVE FOX.

It was of an Earl with an ancient name,
Who hunted the fox, but preferr'd him tame,
Tho' his sire had been a keen hunter free
And bold as e'er rode o'er a grass countree.
That sire once mounted his well-bred horse,
And view'd the fox from the hillside gorse.
His son has come down by a second-class train,
Worried a bagman and home again.

'Tis half-past twelve by the station clocks,
And the Earl has call'd for his horse and fox.
Behind the good Earl there rides a groom,
And next comes a man with a big birch broom,
Wearing the Earl's discarded breeches,
Who will tickle the fox when he comes to the ditches.
The Earl's admirers are ranged in Brown's yard,
They all wear black boots, and mean to ride hard ;
Either wily fox or the timid hare
Be the game to-day, none of them care :
It was well that the Earl had call'd for his fox,
And brought him from Tring in a little deal box.

Three hours or more they drew for a hare,
And drew all in vain, 'twas blank despair ;
Then cried the Earl to the elder Brown,
"Open the box and turn him down."
They turn'd him down in Aylesbury Vale,
In sight of a fence call'd post and rail,
To suit the views of a certain gent
Who rather liked rails and thought he " went."

Over the rails, the first to fly,
Was the jumping gent, but the fox was sly,
And would have declined, but the Earl and his groom,
The Huntsman and Whip, and the man with the broom,
And some boys in a cart, and the Browns, Sam and John,
Would not hear of his shrinking, and urged him on.

THE CAPTIVE FOX.

A pleasant line the captive took,
Avoiding the doubles and shirking the brook ;
As you may imagine he went by rule,
Only taking the fences he learnt at school.
Five hounds of Baron Rothschild's breed,
Unmatch'd for courage and strength and speed,
Close on his flying traces they came,
And almost won the desperate game ;
Just as the Earl prepared to sound
The dread "Whoo Whoop," he went to ground ;
So they dug him out, the Earl and his groom,
The Huntsman and Whip, and the man with the broom.
The fox and the hounds are at Tring again,
And his lordship return'd by the four o'clock train.

The well-known Jem Morgan, who hunted Mr. Conyer's hounds in Essex for some years, was Lord Lonsdale's huntsman, and, although he enjoyed his ride over the fine grass country round Aylesbury, he never could be reconciled to hunting the "Bagman." Poor old Morgan was pensioned off by his lordship, but not long after broke his neck from a fall off his horse while hunting with the Old Berkeley near Chesham. After he fell he remounted his horse, viewed the fox away, gave the "Tally ho!" and followed over two fields, but felt faint, and rode to a neighbouring farmhouse, laid down on a sofa, and, when the doctor came to examine him, he raised himself up, his head fell forward, and he died instantly. He was a rare specimen of a true sportsman, a most courteous man, and as fine a horseman as ever crossed a saddle.

"The noble art of self-defence" has, after some half-century of slumber, apparently revived, but under the milder name of a glove-fight. Probably the science of defence can be as well practised with gloves as with the knuckles, *de puris naturalibus*, and without the brutal punishment. One of the most determined and gallant contests ever fought in modern days (for the details my readers must be referred to the pages of *Bell's Life* of nearly sixty years ago) was a fight for the championship of the light weights, for £500, the combatants being Johnny Broome and Jack Hannan. I am not quite sure, but I think Broome won ; he represented London, whilst Hannan hailed from Birmingham.

The contest took place at the little village of Ambroseden, near Bicester, on the borders of the counties of Bucks and Oxon, and not far from Northamptonshire. My father had just gone on a visit to some agricultural friends in that county, and I, very young then, was for the first time in my life left in charge of our house of business. One evening whilst lounging about with an almost empty house to look after, I was startled by the sudden arrival of an open barouche and four post-horses. The barouche contained four gentlemen who impatiently demanded if they could have beds. They were answered in the affirmative, and on alighting, they expressed their surprise that the house was not full of company. I could not repress my astonishment at their surprise until the strangers informed me that "the great fight" was to come off the very next morning, but that the locality where it was to take place had been kept a strict secret, and that it was not impossible only a very short time would elapse before the house and probably the town of Aylesbury would be crammed with visitors. One of the guests, Lord Walter Butler, ordered dinner, and then they began to deposit with me for safe-keeping their watches, chains, purses, and other valuables, to be retained by me until their return, after the battle.

As they had anticipated, a few minutes after they had spoken, up drove an omnibus drawn by four horses, containing twelve or fourteen hungry travellers all calling together for beds and dinner, and, whilst the well-known old cook of Count D'Orsay fame was taking their several orders, we were apprised of the arrival of another omnibus and four, followed in quick rotation by two more carriages laden with cargoes of the backers of one or other of the champions.

By this time the whole house was filled with noisy sportsmen, and many applicants were sent away for want of accommodation. The great Rochester Room was at once taken possession of, and beds were made up even on the floor, while later comers went off to the other inns in the town, but many who preferred to stop with us had to remain up the whole night long. I should have mentioned that one of the carriages reaching the White Hart contained six barristers who were in the habit of attending the Norfolk Circuit, Aylesbury being then one of the towns in which the Assizes on that circuit were held. Mr. Birch was one, and I think Mr. Byles another, afterwards Serjeant and subsequently Mr. Justice Byles. On my expressing to Mr. Birch my surprise at their presence on such an occasion, he told me very seriously, that they were all averse to seeing a prize-fight, but thought it their duty to witness one, as they often had clients who, having got into difficulties during a prize-fight, afterwards entrusted them with their defence, and they found that they lacked sufficient knowledge to conduct their cases satisfactorily. Anyhow, on business or pleasure bent, there they were, lawyers, lords, and sharpers. I found I had under my charge the *élite* of "The Fancy"—noble lords, Members of Parliament, and men of most of the learned professions. It was even whispered that "the cloth" was represented.

Early in the morning the town of Aylesbury was astir, and every horse I could obtain in the place was requisitioned, while the town was ransacked to supply the visitors with breakfast. The crowd assembled to witness the fight was immense; the Aylesbury contingent hailed from London, but others came in vast numbers from Birmingham, *viâ* Banbury and Bicester, and these exceeded in numbers the Southerners. The fight was a gallant one, and the scene was devoid of all the disgusting brutality that has usually been attributed to these battles. After nearly eighty rounds had been fought out, one of the combatants came forward and shook hands with his opponent, and confessed he had had enough, and was fairly beaten, and not a single hitch occurred to mar the exhibition of a splendid display of science, pluck, and endurance.

Some amusing episodes occurred during the day. One friend of mine, a leading farmer in the neighbourhood of Bicester, attended the fight on horseback, and some men, who were pressed upon by his horse, earnestly entreated him to take charge of a poor little boy, about twelve years old, who, they said, was being nearly crushed to death. My friend kindly permitted them to put the lad up behind his saddle; he told the boy to put his arms round him and to hold on tight. The boy did so, and, when near the close of the fight, the men heartily thanked my friend for his kindness to their kinsman, and, lifting the innocent little lad down, were soon lost sight of. The rider then discovered that his watch and purse were gone, and every farthing of money he had, nearly £20. The poor little fellow had managed to rummage the farmer's pockets with eminent success.

Of course these pugilistic encounters brought together crowds of thieves and scoundrels of every description, and the districts in which the contests took place were often pillaged wholesale. The proprietor of the King's Arms at Bicester lost nearly all his plate, about £100 worth, while several inns in Aylesbury were also sadly plundered. The Bull's Head Inn lost nearly all the takings of the day, about £25, which was stolen from the desk. The Crown Inn lost £20 in plate, and about the same in money, and minor depredations were the order of the day. It was my good luck to lose nothing whatever; perhaps it was that I had only the cream of the visitors, and the plunderers thought it better to keep away from the "upper ten," some of whom at least would probably have known them well enough as doubtful customers, and in self-defence would have denounced them. The police had been carefully informed beforehand that the fight was sure to take place at Brackley, about twenty miles distant, on the borders of Northamptonshire. They therefore attended at that place in large numbers, so that the battle at Ambroseden proceeded undisturbed by the guardians of the peace. It is curious that the police seemed always the last body to get wind of the real locality to be honoured by being made the site of a pugilistic encounter.

CHAPTER XIII.

The Vienna Exhibition of 1873—A Sturdy English Watch—The Emperor admires my Bull—A Contrast in Costume—The Paris Exhibition of 1878—Four-horned Sheep—Rosa Bonheur visits the Cattle—Foot-and-Mouth Disease—The Projected Palestine Canal—*The Times* condemns it—Its Route, its Cost, its Future.

To myself some of the most pleasant recollections of my life relate to my official connection with the Vienna Exhibition of 1873, and the Paris Exhibition of 1878. I had offered to assist in getting up a representative section of English live stock in connection with the "Welt-Ausstellung" at Vienna, and Mr. Philip (now Sir Philip) Cunliffe Owen accepted my assistance. With the exception of cattle, we obtained an excellent entry. The cattle entry consisted entirely of shorthorns; I entered a young bull, "Royal Geneva," one year and ten months old, and his own brother and a red heifer of the Bates "Secrecy" tribe; but our most distinguished breeders were deterred by the distance and the dread of cattle disease. We secured an excellent exhibit of sheep and pigs: Mr. Treadwell sent sheep of his Oxfordshire Down breed, and some Berkshire pigs of the small white variety; Lord Chesham his splendid Shropshire Downs, R. Russell his Kentish, W. Dudding his Lincolns, R. Swannick his Cotswolds, and Lords Sondes and Walsingham their magnificent Southdowns. These were all fine specimens of our flocks. Mr. Duckering sent his large white breed of pigs, and myself and several exhibitors Berkshires and other varieties.

It was no easy matter to select herdsmen for so long a journey. I had arranged that my herdsman, a fine tall specimen of a Highlander, should take charge of my cattle, and act as a sort of head-man over the others. He had prepared to don his full Highland costume; but just before he started he received an advantageous offer from Mr. Tait, the manager of the Queen's show farm, to return to her Majesty's service, and I was reluctantly obliged to waive my hope of exhibiting to the denizens of Vienna the dignified presence and martial costume of this gaunt Scotchman. Mr. Cook, who engaged to convey the precious live freight to its destination, provided an interpreter, a word my men converted into a "terminator."

I was accompanied by Mr. Kirbell, Lord Chesham's farm-steward, who had never before been out of England. We arrived at about 11 p.m. at Cologne. The next morning I wanted to show my friend the cathedral and other places of interest, as I had been there before on more than one occasion. I took out my watch to alter the time and set it by the cathedral clock, as it was quite an hour out, being set to London time. Mr. Kirbell stoutly refused to tamper with the hands of his timepiece; he "was sure these foreign clocks were all wrong," he had had his watch for nearly twenty years, and had never altered it, and he would not do it then.

VIENNA EXHIBITION.

In vain did I try to explain to him, that the further he went eastward the more his time would require correction. No argument would induce him to budge, and when at Vienna, I found he had risen at unearthly hours and perambulated about the city alone, having persisted in being guided by his watch, stoutly asserting that these d——d foreign clocks were all wrong. Kirbell was very anxious also to keep a record of all the places he visited, and always jotted down in his pocket-book the names of the various stations we had stopped at, or passed; after some time he said, "How curious it is there are so many stations of the same name!" I replied that I had not observed it. He showed me his record to prove he was right, and sure enough I found over and over again the word "Ausgang," which he had confidently entered as the name of many stations we had passed on the route.

Arrived at Vienna, and comfortably housed through Sir Philip Cunliffe Owen's kind forethought, I proceeded to see after the arrangement of our English contingent of live beasts under the shedding of the show-building. A small colony of Hungarians were located just outside. The cattle they exhibited were fine large animals of a dark mouse-colour, rather hard in skin, with great spreading horns, the cows not good milkers, scarcely giving more milk than enough to keep their calves. The men were clad in the picturesque costume of their country, and were a fine, sturdy set of fellows.

When the exhibition was opened, the Emperor Franz Joseph first visited this Hungarian colony, and then entered the general exhibition, attended by a numerous suite and by the principal managers of the show, chief amongst whom was the Baron Schwarz Senborn, a most courteous gentleman, with a cheerful manner, which won the good opinion of all with whom he was brought in contact. I had the honour of being introduced to the Emperor, who was very anxious to see the English animals, especially the shorthorns. Surrounded by the Court, he first passed through the sheep department, and was much pleased with Mr. Russell's and Mr. Dudding's Longwools, and Lords Walsingham's and Sondes' Southdowns, but was chiefly struck with the beauty of Lord Chesham's Shropshires, which he examined carefully and declared his admiration of. On arriving at the shorthorns he expressed astonishment at the size and character of my bull "Royal Geneva," and asked to see him led out for inspection; he said he was not surprised at the renown the English shorthorns had attained, when he saw the specimens England had sent to the Exhibition. His uncle, the Archduke Albrecht, who himself is a great breeder of shorthorns, also declared himself greatly pleased with my bull, which eventually obtained the first prize. My man in charge was much elated by the success, in which he claimed to share, and boasts, even now, that "he is the only man in England who ever led out a bull for an Emperor to look at."

I was struck with the picturesque costumes of the men and women in charge of the cattle. Here were Tyrolese peasants in gay costumes, bright ribbons in their hats, in velvet jackets richly embroidered; their women in short white petticoats, scarlet or black velvet jackets, with charming head-dresses, scarlet stockings, black shoes and steel buckles. It was amusing to see these young women literally with one hand "taking the bull by the horns," and with the other holding a short cord from his nostrils, leading him out and walking him round the ring with as much ease as our own men could with assistance of stick and ring. Here also were Austrians and Hungarians in even more brilliant garb; Swiss peasants with their wives tending their silver-grey cattle—cattle so good in quality and appearance, that Mr. Robert Russell, of Kentish renown, bought several, and brought them home to England. Sclavonians there were, Galicians, Italians, Bohemians, and many from Eastern countries bordering on Turkey, Russians of unmistakeable Tartar physiognomy, all in their native dresses, and forming an ethnological group of rare interest to any student of Nature's races. I could not help contrasting the untidy, rough, and slovenly appearance of our cattle-men and shepherds with the smartness and picturesque appearance of their continental brethren. The usual fustian jacket, corduroy trousers, billycock hat, and sometimes a smart but not over clean smock frock, could not have impressed the foreigners with a sense of the boasted superiority of our race.

Some excellent specimens of Austrian cattle were shown, many of the native breeds being sensibly improved by judicious crossing with our best strains, and the pure shorthorns belonging to the Archduke Albrecht, sprung directly from our Queen's Knightley and Booth herd, were wonderfully good; indeed the Archduke's fat cattle were fit for any of our Christmas exhibitions at Birmingham or Islington.

I sold the prize bull and a heifer for 2,000 florins to Count Polanowski from Galicia—1,400 florins for the bull, and 600 for the heifer. It was very fortunate for me that I did not trust to the auction sale, for the prices obtained were simply absurd; after several animals had been knocked down at less that butcher's prices, the remainder were withdrawn, and the cattle show of " Welt-Ausstellung" at Wien was brought to an end. Nearly all the sheep, however, from England sold at good prices; some few were returned to Stettin and disposed of there; but one conclusion I arrived at was, that it is a mistake to take cattle of highly-distinguished lineage to continental shows—good shapely animals, plenty of flesh, with full pedigrees, but of any mixture of tribes, which in England make but ordinary prices, will prove possibly remunerative at such places; but woe betide a breeder if he depends on his Duchess, his Oxford, his Knightley, or his Booth blood, as the foreign buyer knows nothing of the way in which fashion rules the price with us.

I must not forget to add that Mr. Kirbell's watch stuck to its English time in spite of every change of latitude, and on his arrival on British soil proved to be within a minute of Greenwich time.

In the year 1878 it was proposed by the French Government that an exhibition of Cattle and Poultry should be held during the months of May and June, in connection with the great international gathering in Paris. The Royal Agricultural Society of England was consulted, and the Council undertook to co-operate, and were somewhat tardily assisted by the then English Government. The late Sir Brandeth Gibbs was appointed by the Society to superintend the entries, and to make arrangements for the due conveyance of the cattle and poultry and the management and feeding whilst at the Exhibition, and I received a formal appointment to assist him.

The collection of cattle, sheep, and pigs was an excellent one, and consisted of about sixty shorthorns, fifty Highland, Polled Angus, and other Scotch breeds, and twenty-five Herefords and longhorns. Her Majesty contributed a large number of shorthorn cattle. The Marquis of Exeter, Lord Bective, Lady Pigot, Mr. Fox, myself, and other shorthorn breeders sent several other fine specimens. The Queen also sent Devons, and Mr. Fryer Sussex. The Scots were nobly represented by Mr. M'Combie, Sir Macpherson Grant, and Mr. Duncan. The Duke of Buckingham and Mr. Farmer contributed excellent longhorns, and Mr. Robertson, of Dublin, Little Kerries from Ireland. There were no Alderneys or Jerseys, and only a single Ayrshire. The sheep were a good lot, Oxfordshires, Kentish, Dorset, and the "race Jonas Webb," as our friends across the Channel still persist in calling our Southdowns. It is curious how some of the original names of sheep, which they bore when introduced into France many years ago, still adhere to them—the " race Dishley," longwools, when crossed become " Dishley Merinos," " Dishley Artesiennes," " Southdown Merinos," " Southdown Dishley."

Some remarkably curious sheep were pointed out to me, as illustrating a paper read by me some time before at the Farmers' Club on the "Influence of the Male Animal in externals in breeding." A Mr. Isaac Watts, who resided near Devizes, had a desire to produce a breed of sheep with four horns; the Dorsets having only two large curling horns on the head. Whilst he was in South America he had seen some four-horned mountain sheep, and succeeded in bringing to England a four-horned ram. His first cross with his Dorset flock produced all four-horned sheep, and he succeeded in establishing the type. These sheep were fine specimens, and the head of the original imported four-horned ram was stuffed and preserved, and exhibited in the pen over the progeny.

Nearly every day his Royal Highness the Prince of Wales came to look at the live-stock department, and took the keenest interest in its arrangements. He thoroughly identified himself with the well-being of the undertaking, and to his advice not a little of its success was due. The final decision of the premier prize given for the best group or collection of cattle exhibited was anxiously awaited. After a keen competition the prize was finally adjudicated to Mr. M'Combie's beautiful Polled Angus, her Majesty and the Marquis of Exeter with their shorthorns coming next. I was content with only an "honourable mention" for my heifer "Graffin Foggathorpe," but I was compensated by winning the gold medal for the best collection of poultry.

I recollect a curious incident which took place at the close of the show. Sir Philip Owen came to me one day and said some people had been to ask if he could arrange for the letting of Mr. James Duncan's fine Highland bull for six months. I was much surprised at the demand, as I wondered why this animal should be required to improve the "Charolais" and other noted French breeds, but as Mr. Duncan had left Paris I wrote to ask his terms. He replied, "Fifty guineas for *the hire* for six months, and one hundred and fifty guineas for the animal if bought outright." The next day Sir Philip called round with a rather ordinary-looking oldish French lady, and said the animal was not required for breeding, but as a model for the lady accompanying him, who was no other than Madame Rosa Bonheur. The little dame, who scarcely spoke a word of English, said, if it could be arranged, she wished the bull sent direct to her studio at Fontainebleau. Mr. Duncan was again written to, and replied that Madame Bonheur might have the bull for nothing, and that he was only too happy to have his herd immortalized by so great an artist, and I saw the animal safely despatched to its novel destination. I have since seen at M. Lefèvre's gallery a remarkably grand portrait of this bull, who now figures in many of Madame's pictures of Highland cattle and scenery. Mr. Duncan told me that some time afterwards he had received a splendid portrait of his animal in Rosa Bonheur's most perfect style.

It is a melancholy tale to tell of the conclusion of this great undertaking, that on our return to England I discovered that we had brought back with us the dreaded "foot-and-mouth" disease. Nearly one-half of the cattle either died or were slaughtered at Brown's Wharf on the Thames, and several thousand pounds were sacrificed by this heavy misfortune. I have no doubt whatever that the Rinderpest, Pleuro-Pneumonia, and Foot-and-Mouth Disease are unmistakeably of foreign origin. As, and until Mr. Chaplin became Minister for Agriculture, the Government of the day were loth to grapple with this dreadful scourge, some of the leading farmers formed a society called "The Home Cattle Defence Association," and that well-known leader of the agriculturists, Jno. Clayden of Littlebury was appointed chairman, and myself vice-chairman. The principle which we supported was, that "all imported cattle should be slaughtered at the port of debarkation"; and this being persistently insisted on, was at length made the foundation of all our cattle-disease legislation. Of course we were denounced as in reality only advocating protection in disguise; but when we proved that the loss to Great Britain during these outbreaks had been more than ten millions sterling, people began to see it was a national question.

Amongst the projects with which I have been connected, none has interested me so much as that of the Palestine Canal. Mr. Henley, an old Indian engineer, asked me to act on the Board of Directors, and assist in trying to accomplish this gigantic undertaking. After full consultation with Hobart Pacha, Sir Henry Layard, Admiral Inglefield, and others whose opinions were of value, we managed to form a syndicate, with the Duke of Sutherland at its head, with a small capital of £10,000, to provide funds for a survey and report. I believe Lord Dufferin was then in Cairo, and undertook to superintend the management of the surveyors and engineers; but a first blow to the proposal was the foul murder of Palmer and his companion on or near the district to be surveyed; then came the news that the Arabs would massacre any one who appeared on the territory, and Lord Dufferin had to withdraw the survey for the time, and the fortunes of the scheme began to wane. My friend, Mr. Henley, then became dangerously ill, and as he was an old man of seventy-three or seventy-four, he made over to me the entire management on his behalf.

A powerful article in *The Times* appeared, strongly condemnatory of the proposed canal, and making a point of its destroying, if ever completed, all the most sacred spots of Holy Scripture—the river Jordan, the Dead Sea, the city of Jericho, and other sites consecrated in history. I replied, the next day, in the same paper, that if it were *un fait accompli*, the canal would not do the injury to sacred sentiment that the Suez Canal had done, as that great work had entirely destroyed the recorded Passage of the Israelites through the Red Sea; that many other events had taken place in modern times of the same character, which had been conducive to the advance of civilization.

I may perhaps, as briefly as possible, give the general outlines of the scheme. There are two forks to the Red Sea, one forming the Gulf of Suez, the other the Gulf of Akabah. From the latter is a remarkable depression, about twenty miles from the sea, which rapidly falls a depth of 1300 feet to the Dead Sea, and this depression is continued for the whole distance through the valley of the river Jordan, and then slowly rises up to the Sea of Tiberias. This valley is in parts twelve or fourteen miles wide; on the western side stands the city of Jerusalem, which, at present, is 2000 feet above the valley and the Dead Sea. Mr. Henley's plan was to cut a channel about sixty yards wide, for about twenty miles from the top of the Gulf of Akabah, and let in the waters of the Red Sea ; and, as the whole country from thence to the Dead Sea is a loose sandy gravel, it would wash out its own course to the inland sea and rapidly submerge it. The river Jordan rises many miles to the north of this sea, and flows into it, and the waters would fill the valley on each side of the river, and continue to do so up to the Sea of Tiberias. At the Mediterranean end from the Gulf of Acre, it would pass down the valley of Esdraelon, submerging the brook Kedron, and through a cutting of twenty-seven miles from near Mount Carmel, would join the valley of the Jordan about thirty miles south of the Lake of Tiberias. Here the waters of the Mediterranean would rapidly assist in filling up the valley, and meet the waters of the Red Sea.

Mr. Henley computed that it would take three years for the two seas to fill the enormous natural depression, and that upwards of 736,272,000,000 of cubic yards of water would be required for the purpose. Jerusalem is now 2000 feet above the Jordan, but if the Palestine Canal were completed, it would only be 700 feet above it, and less than ten miles from the canal, and would probably become an important port. The plain on which Damascus stands is one of the most fertile in the world. The city itself contains a population of 110,000 souls, and a continuous stream of pilgrims pass from the city and its neighbourhood to Mecca. With the development of the productive soil, it was computed that an enormous amount of traffic would find its way to the canal, and pass out either to the Indies or to the Mediterranean ports.

The estimates for this remarkable work varied from twenty-five millions to fifty millions sterling. The Suez Canal is believed to have cost over forty millions; but 55 per cent. of its earnings have to be expended in dredging the channel, and keeping its ports open from the immense accumulation of sand. Besides which, after all, it is a mere ditch, and at any time an accident might stop the whole traffic, whereas, in the Palestine Canal, the channel would be of great depth and width—in some places twelve to fourteen miles wide—and sailing-ships of the largest size could easily navigate throughout its entire length.

In the end the Syndicate which was at that time formed (1884) resolved to wait until a more certain survey could be formed, especially at the Akabah end of the canal, and up to the present time the scheme has been in abeyance; but I firmly believe that some day this gigantic project will eventually be carried out, and will do more to enlarge the power and influence of England in the East than any suggestion that has as yet been made.

CHAPTER XIV.

Posting on the Great North Road—Bob Newman of Regent Street —Old "Boys"—Loyal Tom King of Amersham ; he drives King George III.—An Elopement and the Sequel—May-Day Procession of the Mails—The Railway Fiend—The Wisdom of Weller—Old London Inns—An English Bill of Fare and the *Menu à la Russe*—The Old Norfolk Circuit—The Bar Mess : Fitzroy Kelly *v.* Serjeant Storks—One Pint many Times— Puritan Ipswich—A Peccant Engine.

IN my early childhood and boyhood the old modes of travelling by post-horses and stage-coaches had been brought to great perfection, and the pace at which the public then travelled seemed incredible to a former generation—in fact, the arrangements for the different lines of posting on the main arteries out of London almost deserved the name of a fine art. The practice of what was called "running in money" was the system of paying post-boys a certain sum of money as a premium for bringing a carriage with either a pair or four horses to the first change. For instance, we will take Barnet as our starting-point, which was the first station on the great North Road. This small town, like nearly all those on the whole route, had two rival posting-establishments, and each establishment had its own line of posting-houses the whole way to York, Chester, or wherever it might be. The *boys*—often very old post-boys—had on each line distinctive costumes; either the blue or buff jackets, and either white or black top-hats, the white generally with the blue, and the black with the buffs; and it was very rarely that a gentleman, travelling in his own carriage for more than a hundred miles, if he once got on to the blue line, ever got off it till he arrived at his destination. It was all essential, therefore, to get possession of the carriage for the first stage, and, when competition was keen, a post-boy at Barnet would have 10*s.* given him by the post-master for bringing *a job*, as it was called; and when the carriage arrived at the next change the same post-boy would bring back from the second post-master 7*s.* 6*d.*, and at the next 5*s.* would be sent back, and at the fourth 2*s.* 6*d.* would be returned; so the 10*s.* paid by the first post-master was divided between himself and the next three, and by this time the carriage and its occupants had got fairly on to the main line of either posting-houses.

It was very rarely that there was a third house in any town. Old "Bob Newman," of Regent Street, was the great man for London, and even now the remains of his establishment may be seen on the road to the Derby, with the four greys and the blue-jacketed and white silk hatted post-boys, bumping the saddle like real old times. At many of the first stages out of London very large establishments were kept. The two rival houses at Barnet each kept from twenty to thirty pairs of post-horses; Hounslow, Uxbridge, and the houses on great roads to the Eastern counties and to Dover did the same. The usual charge was 1*s.* 6*d.* per mile for a pair of horses, and 3s. for four horses; the post-boys were paid something over 3d. per mile; and as there were generally two turnpike gates, often three, between every stage, at a charge of 9d. to 1s. per pair, this, in addition to the tip of 6d. to the ostler at each stage, brought the cost of posting to about 2s. per mile. The old yellow post-chaise, immortalized by Caldecott, and generally seen in elopements, had one seat for two people inside, and a small "dickey," as it was called, in front, where the gentleman's valet could ride. This gave way to the post-chariot, with box-seat holding two, for the valet and lady's maid; in turn the post-chariot was supplanted by the fly, which held four inside, and threw open, with a lofty box-seat, and conveyed six people. Soon after the pair of horses began to disappear, and the "one-horse fly" became the fashion, to the horror of the old-fashioned post-master and his old boys. The introduction of the railways put a stop to all this system, posting has degenerated into a fly to and from the station, and this aristocratic species of locomotion has become a thing of the past.

Dickens makes the immortal Sam Weller say, "Nobody ever saw a dead post-boy or dead donkey," and the longevity of the former was proverbial; although their lives were passed out in all weathers, oftentimes all night through, with constant liquoring up at roadside public-houses, yet they were a healthy, hardy race. Arrived at the end of a stage they groomed their horses, washed their legs, unharnessed and fed them with a good feed of hay, chaff, and corn at the charge of 1s., and 2d. for ostler, and the boys went indoors and had, free of cost, a good meal, a pint of beer, and glass of hot grog before they departed, provided by the landlord of the inn. My father had an old boy, Humphrey by name, known far and near, whose age no one could make out, but he lived at the White Hart for more than forty years, and bumped the saddle to the last. Elderly ladies selected him for his care and civility, but he also could put a pair of good stepping horses along at ten to twelve miles an hour among the best of them.

When poor Henry Dixon, " The Druid," once visited me, I told him a tale of a post-boy which so pleased him that he introduced it into his book of *Saddle and Sirloin*, and it was selected by *The Times* in their review of his book as one of the best anecdotes of the time. It was this. My grandfather was a tenant of a large farm of Mr. Drake's, of Amersham, and also of the Crown Inn. One morning in the beginning of the century, the usual cry when a "job," as it was called, appeared, of " First turn out " was heard. My grandfather went to the door of a yellow post-chaise, and saw a kindly-looking, benevolent old gentleman sitting in the corner, in hunting costume, who ordered out a chaise and pair to Windsor, which was about fifteen miles off. " The first turn," singularly enough, as events proved, was old Tom King, who quickly got out "the yellow," the old gentleman got in, and was bowled off to Windsor. When Tom returned at night he was greatly excited, and he declared, and it was the truth, that he had been driving the King, George the Third. He had got rather moist on the occasion, and for many years afterwards always asked on the anniversary of the event for a holiday, which he spent sitting in the corner of the post-chaise where the King had sat, smoking his pipe, drinking sundry pots of beer, and treating all comers that they might pledge the King's health; and he enlivened his company, and destroyed the peace of all who heard him, by playing "God save the King" on the key-bugle till late at night, when the beer and smoke began to take effect, and the notes on the bugle got more entangled and fainter, till it ceased altogether. Poor old Tom's loyalty never failed. When he ceased to be a "boy," and had become a pensioner on my family, he was regaled with a good dinner and plenty of ale on each anniversary, but on this condition—that he did not play the key-bugle.

À propros of the old yellow post-chaise, I can just remember a singular adventure. One evening—when a little boy—I was standing in the portico of the White Hart with my father, when a post-chaise and four horses came down the street at a furious rate. On pulling up at the door a handsome, military-looking young gentleman got out, and handed out a charming and beautiful young lady, ordering another chaise and horses out directly. Almost before the order was given, a young gentleman galloped up, jumped off a horse which was covered with foam, seized the first gentleman by the collar, knocked him down, and thrashed him with his riding-whip. The young lady screamed and ran up the street and took refuge in a small public-house. In a few minutes a second chaise and pair came rattling down the street, containing an old gentleman, who jumped out demanding, "Where is my daughter?" A crowd had collected, and my father had not seen in the confusion whither the lady had fled ; but on hearing her whereabouts he went to her, found her in hysterics, and unable to be moved. Her father soon calmed her; meanwhile the gentleman who had been so suddenly assailed had at last struggled on to his feet, and was engaged in a hand-to-hand encounter with his opponent, but was soon separated. The young lady was taken possession of by her father, and returned with him and the younger man who had ridden up in pursuit. The poor young fellow who had eloped with the girl, most disconsolate at her loss, stayed at the house that night, and told my father his story. It appeared that the young lady was engaged to a gentleman she did not care for ; and after he had met her at a ball and at other places at Cheltenham, she became attached to him, and at last agreed to elope with him. A chaise and four was ordered, and before her parents were moving in the morning she left the house with only a handbag. Her lover met her, and they went first to Oxford, intending either to get to London or to the North Road and so on to Gretna Green. To elude pursuit they took post-horses to Thame, instead of keeping on the highroad, and then came on to Aylesbury. Whilst on the turnpike road, they saw a man at the corner of a byeroad breaking stones, and asked him the route. The father and the lady's brother following, singularly enough had pulled up and asked the same man if he had seen a chaise and four pass that way. He told them that about half an hour before one had turned off towards Bicester. My father, who felt much interested in the romantic affair, heard some time afterwards that a hostile meeting had been the result, and that on the sands at Boulogne the brother of the unfortunate lady shot the officer, who died on the spot. These romances of the road are no more. An elopement by the Metropolitan Railway line has not much glamour about it.

Nowadays one of the prettiest sights of the London season are the parades of the "Coaching" and "Four-in-hand" Clubs; but with all their beauty they cannot compare with the old May-Day processions of the mail coaches to St. Martin's-le-Grand. It was my good fortune as a boy to accompany my father, as the guest of Mr. Fagg of Bedfont, the proprietor of the coaches on one of the Western routes, to the yearly banquet given in 1832 by the contractor for his Majesty's mails at his establishment in Millbank. This was the *entrepôt* for the building of the coaches, the harness-making, and all the requisites for the equipment of the mails. There, were assembled all the London coach proprietors, the Chaplins and Horns, the Sherborns, the Nelsons, the Hearnes, the Faggs, *et id genus omne*, men who had each from 600 to 1000 horses at work, who prided themselves on the fact that nowhere in the world were to be found such horses, such coaches, such drivers, or such guards—shoulder to shoulder with many of the *élite* of London's sportsmen and "Knights of the Ribbons," the fathers and grand-sires of the Four-in-hand men of the present day.

After the luncheon the company adjourned to the Embankment, where the mails fully equipped were on view. The coaches and harness were either new or newly painted and furbished, the horses in pink of condition and beauty, the coachmen and guards in new liveries of scarlet and gold, each proprietor vying with his opponent in an endeavour to produce the most perfect turn-out. Critics abounded, and the judges gave the awards unbiassed by any predilections for the teams which passed through their respective districts. The procession started, and dense crowds of spectators thronged the route from Westminster through the Strand, Fleet Street, and Ludgate Hill, by the Old Bailey, to the General Post Office, St. Martin's-le-Grand. Here the mail-bags were loaded, and on such a special occasion nearly every seat for passengers was filled, and off the coaches started on their respective journeys. Well might foreigners exclaim, with the thought of their own lumbering diligences before them, that it was worth travelling to England to see the completeness and style with which the public were conveyed from one part of the kingdom to the other, and the celerity and despatch with which the correspondence of the nation was distributed.

Great opposition was shown by the stage-coach proprietors and post-masters to the innovation of the iron horse; prognostications were lavishly made of the absolute impossibility of the railway competing in pace and safety with the old coach and yellow post-chaise; pamphlets threw doubt on George Stephenson's statement that he could carry passengers at twenty miles an hour, and every effort was made to prevent passengers travelling by the new system. Messrs. Chaplin and Horne alone had the prescience to see that the "old order changeth, yielding place to new," and when the London and Birmingham Railway was near completion they assisted the Company by finding omnibuses and vehicles to meet their trains at Euston, and to convey passengers over the unfinished sections of the line. It was a long time before the exclusiveness of the nobility and of the old country gentlemen was broken through, before they would condescend to mix with those who could not boast their own private carriages; and for some time after the railway lines were opened private carriages were conveyed on trucks, and the owners rode inside them, till the manifest dangers of the system became patent, and they were compelled to put up with the ordinary first-class compartments. It was no less than a social revolution that was silently produced by the levelling tendency of steam locomotion.

The capital embarked in the coaching and carrying business at that time was estimated at many millions of pounds. Men of the present day can form but a small idea of the importance of coaching and posting before railways were perfected. It seemed hard, after Telford, Macadam, and other engineers had laid out and improved the great main roads of the kingdom, and coaching and posting had arrived as near as possible to perfection, that the Stephensons, the Brunels, and Lockes should have cast to the winds the splendid results that had been achieved by the knights of the whip and the road. As an old coach proprietor I must perforce recount a few of the grievances which we country proprietors loved to air. The London firms had many great advantages over us. Every coach that left any booking-office was charged £1 per month for booking passengers, and as many hundred coaches ran into London, at £12 per annum each, it became a very large sum for the Londoners to pocket, amounting to some thousands a year. Each coach was charged 12*s*. 6*d*. a week for washing and greasing the wheels; for every parcel or passenger had to be paid 2*d*. for booking; the coachmen paid their takings into the London end, and thus the London proprietors had thousands always at their bankers. The accounts were made up monthly, and divided at so much per mile for their earnings, and each man who horsed the coach had his mileage sent him, whilst if any loss of parcels or otherwise had happened on his section of the road, he was the person made responsible. At every stage the coachman took what was called his waybill into the office and entered the number of passengers taken up and carried, their fares were placed in the proper column, and the money was given up at the journey's end. The proprietors were thus entirely at the mercy of the coachmen and guards, as there was no check upon the miles the passengers were recorded as having travelled. It was always considered that the government, in duty and taxes, owned one wheel of the coach, and the coachman and guard purloined another wheel, the turnpikes, farriers, harness-makers, and coach-painters had another, which left one wheel only to the proprietors as their share of the profit. Only when the coachman and guard began to "shoulder," as it was called, and took an unexampled pull at the takings, did proprietors wax wroth, and a general dismissal all round took place. It was amusing to watch the way in which the old coachmen of the mails and long stages looked down on the drivers of short stages, and the four-horse men on the pair-horse men. Dickens with capital humour illustrates this by the mouth of the elder Weller to Sam, who in writing his love-letter had ventured on a rhyme; upon which the elder Weller remarked: "It was wery wulgar to write Potry—he never knowed a coachman write Potry, except vun as wrote a most affecting copy o' werses the night afore he vos hung; but then he *vos only a Camberwell man*—so that says nothing"—the Camberwell stages being pair-horse coaches only.

When I was a boy the inhabitants of a country district made the inns where the mails and stage-coaches which served their locality arrived and started from in London their halting-places: thus, the Old Bell Inn, Holborn, was the resort of the residents in Bucks and the adjoining counties; the King's Arms, Snow Hill, for Warwickshire and Northamptonshire; the Spread Eagle, Gracechurch Street, and the Swan with Two Necks accommodated the dwellers in Essex, and other districts had each their favourite house. The Old Bell remains as it was more than fifty years ago, and all who have a desire to see an old London inn should visit the house before it is swept away to make room for the modern improvements which are everywhere changing the aspect of Old London; the Bull, nearly adjoining it, is of the same character, and still awaits the inevitable change. The coffee-room at the Old Bell was carpetless; it had boxes, as they were called, or divisions, each provided with a small table and fixed seats, some holding eight, some six, and some with accommodation only for one or two persons. The cooking, though plain, was excellent; a joint was ready, with a dish of fish, daily about five o'clock, but the country folk generally preferred rump-steak and oyster sauce, with a fried sole, prime ripe cheddar cheese, and a tankard of strong ale, the dinner to wind up with a bottle of undeniably good old crusted port. Then, at seven o'clock, most of the company went off to the play, and, on their return, a score of native oysters with stout, and after this a glass of hot brown brandy and water, prepared the guests for bed. I remember my father taking me and my brother up from the country to see Joey Grimaldi as clown in the pantomime. The lumbering hackney coach and pair of horses afforded us the means of locomotion; cabs had not been introduced, and, until Mr. Shillibeer, that eminent innovator, had bethought him of the omnibus, there was no other way of reaching the destination required except on foot. But the greatest change is in these old-fashioned inns themselves, altered out of all recognition into the modern *hotel*. The first step was the improving and fitting-up of The Castle and Falcon, Aldersgate Street, Bacon's Hotel in Great Queen Street, The Golden Cross, Charing Cross; then new buildings arose, The Queen's or The Bull and Mouth, St. Martin's-le-Grand, which has since disappeared to allow the enlargement of the Post-office; then the railway companies built their station caravansaries, and such structures as the Langham came on the scene; and now of course the hotels of London dwarf the royal palaces and the Houses of Parliament themselves.

I noticed lately in reading Captain Gronow's reminiscences, he remarks upon the inferiority of the dinners at the few clubs which were in existence at the close of the Regency, how the fashionable society of the day preferred dining at the Clarendon, Grillon's, or Limmer's. The change which periodically takes place in the manners and customs of the diner is very noticeable. During the last fifty years there has been a complete alteration, not only in the nature of the viands served up for consumption, but in the serving of them, in the table decorations, in the very furniture of the dining-room. The main feature, which must strike every one, is the decrease in the heavy joints, dishes of fish, rich puddings, and in the old profusion of vegetables, under the weight of which the tables groaned, which have now been replaced by lightness and elegance even in the viands, and by the delicate and tasteful style in which they are now presented to the guests. I might illustrate my meaning by a *menu*, or, as it used to be called, a "Bill of Fare," of the Olden Time. I found it amongst some papers at the White Hart. About twenty guests partook of this dinner, which was given to Lord Blaney by the officers of the Bucks Yeomanry. The chief characteristic, as it appears on the *carte*, is that each course was placed on the table complete—sauces, vegetables, side dishes, or, as we now call them, *entrées*, along with the joints—and everything was carved upon and served from the table, nothing being handed round by the waiters. The manner in which the dishes are noted down on the page is to direct the waiters as to where to place them on the table.

BILL OF FARE.
at 5 p.m.
WHITE HART, AYLESBURY.   THURSDAY, SEPTEMBER 13, 1815.

First Course.
Turtle Soup.
Potatoes.
Lobster Sauce.   Melted Butter.   Lobster Sauce.
Turbot.
Butter.
Potatoes.
Turtle Soup.

Second Course.
Boiled Fowls.
Harricot Mutton.   Oyster Sauce.   Beef Olives.
Tongue.   Turnips and Carrots.
Mint Sauce.
Greens.   Saddle of Lamb.   Stewed Pigeons.
Salad.
Veal Olives.   Boiled Leg of Pork.   French Beans.
Potatoes.   Pease Pudding.   Cauliflower.
Tremlong of Beef.   Roast Fowls.

Third Course.
Sweet Sauce.   Brace of Birds.   Bread Sauce.
Potatoes   Hare.   Potatoes.
(Flowers.)
Bread Sauce.   Hare.   Bread Sauce.
Brace of Birds.

Fourth Course.
Jelly.   Gooseberry Pie.   Blancmange.
Custards.   Baked Apple Pudding.   Apricot Tart.
Apricot Tart.   Plum Pie.   Custards.
Blancmange.   Boiled Plum Pudding.   Fruit in Jelly.
Port.   Sherry.
Claret.   Champagne.
Turtle Punch.

I extract this, as I found it, from the book in which the orders and arrangements for dinners were recorded. From an old account-book I find the bill with wine came to about one pound ten shillings a head. The substantiality of the repast, and the hour at which it was served, are worthy of note, and the boiled leg of pork and pease-pudding; but this was probably a favourite dish of Lord Blaney's. In the same way, at the dinners of the Royal Hunt Club, the standard dishes of "steak and oyster pudding" and "Irish stew" were ordered to be served every day, as Lord Erroll would insist upon these dishes appearing at every dinner of the Hunt.

I notice by an entry in the book I have referred to, that one of the last of these old-fashioned dinners was given by "Squire" Drake to about seventy gentlemen : one of the courses consisted of twenty-six dishes of fish. The dinner *à la Russe* gradually superseded the old English style, even at the Tory White Hart. It had obvious advantages, advantages both æsthetic and from the point of view of practical comfort, but it entails in waiting and decoration a larger degree of expenditure, and lacks something of the hospitality of the former method. It is possible that a combination of the two styles might produce a yet happier result.

The White Hart at Aylesbury being situated close to the Assize Courts, that hostelry became the head-quarters of the lawyers who attended what was at that time the Norfolk Circuit. Most, if not all, the members of the Bar had their lodgings at private houses ; but when the railways began to bring all these gentlemen of the legal profession in a crowd together into the town, the seclusion and exclusiveness of barristers when on circuit was brought to an end, and barristers as well as solicitors began to occupy the hotels, both for lodging and meals, except indeed the leaders, who still kept to their private lodgings.

Between the years 1835 and 1840, Fitzroy Kelly and his friend, Mr. Dasent, were convicted of bribery or some other irregularity in connection with the elections of Yarmouth and Norwich; for this they were fined and imprisoned, and a split ensued amongst certain members of the Circuit, which separated it into two parties, one clique going by the name of "Kelly's," and the other "the Serjeant's"; this latter group being headed by Serjeant Storks, with Serjeant Byles, of "Byles on Bills" fame, as coadjutor. The White Hart was selected for the Bar mess of the Serjeant's party, which eventually swallowed up the rival faction. Aylesbury came first on the Circuit, and in the charming grounds of the hotel the members of the Bar were accustomed to meet the magistracy and solicitors and their friends.

Of course at the Bar and Quarter Sessions dinners many a good story was told. A woman was tried at Quarter Sessions one day for robbing a man at Aston Clinton. They were at a public-house together, when the female picked the pocket of the man, who bore the aristocratic name of Montague. Mr. Mordaunt Wells (afterwards Mr. Serjeant and finally Sir Mordaunt, and a Judge in India) cross-examined the prosecutor, endeavouring to prove to the best of his ability that the man was drunk. He questioned him as to his consumption of beer. "How many pints did you have whilst in the tap-room?" "Only one," answered Montague. Mr. Wells demanded if he would swear he had not had ten pints. He would swear he hadn't. "Will you swear you had not nine or eight?" Still came the denial; then followed the usual brow-beating, from seven to six, even to four. Whereupon Montague said, "It's no use your bothering me about how many pints I had; I'll swear I had but one, but how many times it was filled I can't say." Amidst loud laughter Mr. Wells ceased his cross-examination.

On another occasion, the day after a private dinner at my house, Mr. Newton, the Marlborough Street chief magistrate, asked Mr. Charles Merewether how the late Hillam Mills, who was fond of a good glass of wine, got on after the wine was on the table? "Oh! very well," he answered, "he helped himself as usual every time the port came to him and never passed the claret." Poor old Hillam Mills, he was truly a boon companion; once when I was visiting him at his residence near Ipswich, he took me in a fly to call on the Lord Chief Baron, who lived at The Chantry, a house near the town. I asked the driver if he was a voter for the borough? "No," he replied in the sing-song vernacular of the Eastern Counties, "I wish I was. I've only a vote for the Coperation, and I only gets half-a-crown for my vote there, and I should have a sovereign if I was a woter for the Borough." This clenched an argument I was having with Mills about the value of the franchise, which at that time was the burning political question of the day.

A RAILWAY CASE.

Some years ago an action was tried at the Assizes at Aylesbury which excited great interest in the railway world. The action was brought by Sir Thos. F. Fremantle, afterwards Lord Cottesloe, to recover damages from the London and North-Western Railway Co. for setting on fire the farm-buildings on his estate at Swanbourne, adjoining the Buckinghamshire Railway, which was owned and worked by the larger company. It was alleged that the sparks from an engine passing along the line from Bletchley to Oxford and Banbury had caused the ignition, and damages to the value of the buildings was claimed thereon. For some years past the railway companies throughout England had been subjected to these actions, and considerable sums had been paid in consequence. This was a test case, that the legal question should be set at rest once and for all, and that the point should be settled as to whether a railway company was answerable for damage from their engines when working on the line, if the company had taken every precaution that human skill could accomplish, not only in working the traffic, but in the building of their locomotives, and had availed themselves of every opportunity that science and invention could suggest in order to be as perfect in every detail as possible.

Sir T. Fremantle's party asserted and proved that a spark from an engine passing down the line had alighted on the thatched roof of one of the farm-buildings and had set on fire and burnt down the property, therefore, they argued, the company were liable for the negligence and carelessness of the driver in charge of the engine.

The case of the company was, that the engine was so constructed that if it did emit sparks, they were innocuous, as they dispersed in the atmosphere before they descended. Eminent engineers proved that they had carefully examined the engine in question, and that it was of the highest class of construction, was almost a new one; and that as the Legislature had granted them an Act of Parliament to construct the line of railway, it also compelled the company to run trains for passengers and goods at stated fares and rates, and that, having taken every precaution to have their engines constructed efficiently, they were not liable. Mr. O'Malley, Q.C., who was counsel for Sir T. Fremantle, cross-examined the great authority, Mr. Fairbairn. After his evidence, which was concise and very conclusive for the company, Mr. O'Malley said, "Well, sir, then you mean to say that this engine was built with all the skill that human ingenuity could suggest?" "Yes!" "That it was impossible—absolutely impossible—for it to emit sparks that could burn down a building?" Mr. Fairbairn said, "Yes, except from the greatest carelessness on the part of the stoker!" Mr. O'Malley turned round immediately to the Judge, and said, "I submit, my lord, that the evidence of the defendants' witness fully establishes our case. If yourself and the jury are satisfied that these buildings were destroyed by a spark from the engine, it shows there was great carelessness on the part of the servants of the defendants, and I therefore claim the verdict." The learned judge summed up, and the jury gave a verdict for the plaintiff.

Some weeks afterwards the locomotive superintendent

of the line called upon me, and, in conversation about the trial, said that the evidence of their own witnesses had been absolutely correct, that it was quite impossible for *that* engine to have set fire to any place ; " but," he said, " the buildings were burnt by the sparks of another of our engines, which had gone up the line a few minutes before the one in question ; and this fact I knew perfectly, and so did the drivers of the engines all through the trial ! " · The jury's verdict, as so often is the case, though wrong on the actual strict facts of the case before them, was just in substance.

CHAPTER XV.

Shorthorn Breeding—The Bates Dinners—Lord Dunmore to the Rescue—Eminent Breeders in the Palmy Days—My Sale and Sales in General—The Rose of the Quarter Sessions—A Dissertation on Poultry—The Prebendal Geese—The Aylesbury Duckling—A Year of Wet and a Year of War—A Legal Decision on Crops.

FOR many years I was prominently associated with the fascinating pursuit of shorthorn cattle breeding. The shorthorn world was divided into two schools, the Bates and Booth admirers. My delight in the Knightley or Fawsley breed, a strain of great purity established by Sir Charles Knightley, of Fawsley in Northamptonshire, had induced me to throw in my lot with the former tribe.

The last chapter partook of the nature of a gastronomical treatise, but I cannot refrain from supplementing its narrative by some mention of the Bates dinners, banquets given by the leaders of those gentlemen who fostered that distinguished line of beasts. They had their origin in a very singular event. Mr. Robartes possessed an excellent herd of cattle, which had become distinguished for their style and quality, and he had been using a highly-bred Bates bull, Duke of Tregunter, of the purest Duchess blood, which he had purchased of Col. Gunter, of Wetherby. After using him a short time, the bull proved to be worthless for stock purposes, and he was advertised to be sold with a large draft of other cattle from Mr. Robartes' herd. It became known that there was a design by some unscrupulous people to buy this bull for apparent use in their herds, and so obtain for the stock a fictitious value; and when The Duke was put up for sale, an animated contest took place. To the surprise of a number of Bates men present, the animal was bought by Lord Dunmore for 155 guineas. In less than half an hour the bull had ceased to exist; his lordship sold him at once to a butcher, and had him killed on the premises, so that no pretence should be made of his services. As the value of the bull for butcher's purposes was not more than twenty-five guineas, Lord Dunmore would have been a great loser by the transaction had not the Bates men present been so pleased with his pluck that a subscription was at once got up, and a considerable sum beyond the purchase-money raised and presented to Lord Dunmore, who, after recouping himself the outlay, provided a most excellent dinner to the leading followers of the Bates blood.

This was the first of the annual Bates dinners. Splendid entertainments they were. Lord Feversham gave his at the St. James's Hotel, the Duke of Devonshire at his own house; but critics preferred, perhaps of all the series, the banquet to which we Bates men were invited by the Marquis of Exeter to partake of at the Albion, in Aldersgate Street. I have by me a list of those who sat down to enjoy the hospitality of Lord Skelmersdale, now Earl of Lathom, on May 1st, 1872, at the Clarendon Hotel; and they represent perhaps some of the most noted breeders of shorthorns, when shorthorn breeding was in its palmiest days. I find there were present Lord Skelmersdale (in the chair), and the Earl of Dunmore (the vice-chairman), the Duke of Devonshire, Mr. Sartoris, Lord Braybrooke, Mr. Cheney of Gaddesby, Mr. Tredcroft, the Earl of Feversham, Mr. Larking, Mr. Foster of Kilhow, Mr. T. Brassey, M.P., Mr. Beauford, Colonel Kingscote, M.P., Lord Penrhyn, Mr. E. Bowley, Captain Oliver, Mr. A. Robartes, Mr. Mackinstosh, Mr. Angerstein, M.P., Mr. Sheldon of Brailes, the Earl of Bective, Mr. Samuda, M.P., and myself.

The value of shorthorns has become much reduced since then; animals which then made thousands of pounds would now scarcely realize as many hundreds.

No sketch of the state of agriculture would be complete without some allusion to the extraordinary mania, as it may fairly be called, which existed about this period of 1870 for shorthorn cattle breeding, and the incredible prices obtained by some of the ashionably-bred tribes, especially of the Bates and Knightley lines. In my account of the Vienna exhibition I have mentioned my bull, Royal Geneva, and the price it fetched. At my sale in 1874, a young cow, Princely, made 125 guineas; Spicey Lightburne 120 guineas; Knightley V. 115 guineas; my heifer calf, Kentish Nonsuch, sixteen months old, made 175 guineas; Charming Knightley, nine months old, I sold to the Duke of Manchester for 175 guineas; Charming Geneva, seven months old, fetched 125 guineas; my heifer calves making an average of £131 5s. each. These were prices which made shorthorn breeding pay. At this same sale Lord Chesham gave 100 guineas for Secrecy, a three-year-old heifer, considered by some, but not by me, a doubtful breeder. Three years afterwards, at his lordship's sale, Lord Fitzhardinge gave 400 guineas for her, and the heifer with which at my sale she was in calf by King Charming, made 275 guineas, and the calf then by her side 115 guineas; so that, on the outlay of 100 guineas, in two years she made a profit of nearly 800 guineas for Lord Chesham!

Those who have not gone deeply into the science and practice of breeding cannot appreciate the pleasure and excitement a breeder experiences when, at a first-class shorthorn sale-ring, under the direction of the veteran "Strafford," or the blandishments of the courteous John Thornton, one of a noted tribe enters the ring, the pedigree is recited through a line of duchesses, culminating either in the renowned J. Brown's, Old Red Bull, or the noted Hubback. The bidding commences by hundreds or by a thousand. "Going, going! Ah! you nearly lost it, sir."—" 2,500," " 2,600 "—" Thank you, sir—and fifty" ("Bravo," from the crowd); " 2,700 in two places"; "and fifty." "Thank you, my lord," and so on till 3,000 is passed, and, the biddings still increasing, the glass slowly runs out, the word "gone" is uttered, and my Lord Fitzhardinge is declared the buyer of the bull at 4,500 guineas. Such was the sum actually realized for Duke of Connaught, at Lord Dunmore's sale in 1875, the largest sum ever reached in England at a public sale of shorthorns. There were, indeed, plucky breeders then. I had the pleasure of paying a visit to Underley to see the sixth Duchess of Oneida, a cow for which Lord Bective had given 3,500 guineas in America, and her splendid deep-red bull calf, Duke of Underley. No breeder of my day, unless it be the Earl of Dunmore, has ever shown the spirit of enterprise more than the Earl of Bective.

My Knightley blood always stood me in good stead, and so long as I could make from 150 to 200 guineas each for yearling heifers, I had no cause to grumble. I think the best and most useful purchase I ever made was by my giving 50 guineas for a three weeks old white bull calf, King Charming, one of the Bates and Charmer tribe. I used him for three years with success, and then sold him to an eminent dairy farmer near Aylesbury for 120 guineas. Nothing can be more disheartening to breeders than the wretched prices which shorthorns have lately made at sales; the thousands have dropped to hundreds, and the hundreds to twenties, and it is now a rarity to find a sale at which the average is more than forty guineas, whereas mine, which had no pretensions to rank with many others, ran to an average of £104 each, and Lord Dunmore's realized over 540 guineas each.

The ingenuity with which Hodge and his *confrères* managed to twist the names of my cattle used to amuse me. I had a cow called Alberta, but my man per-

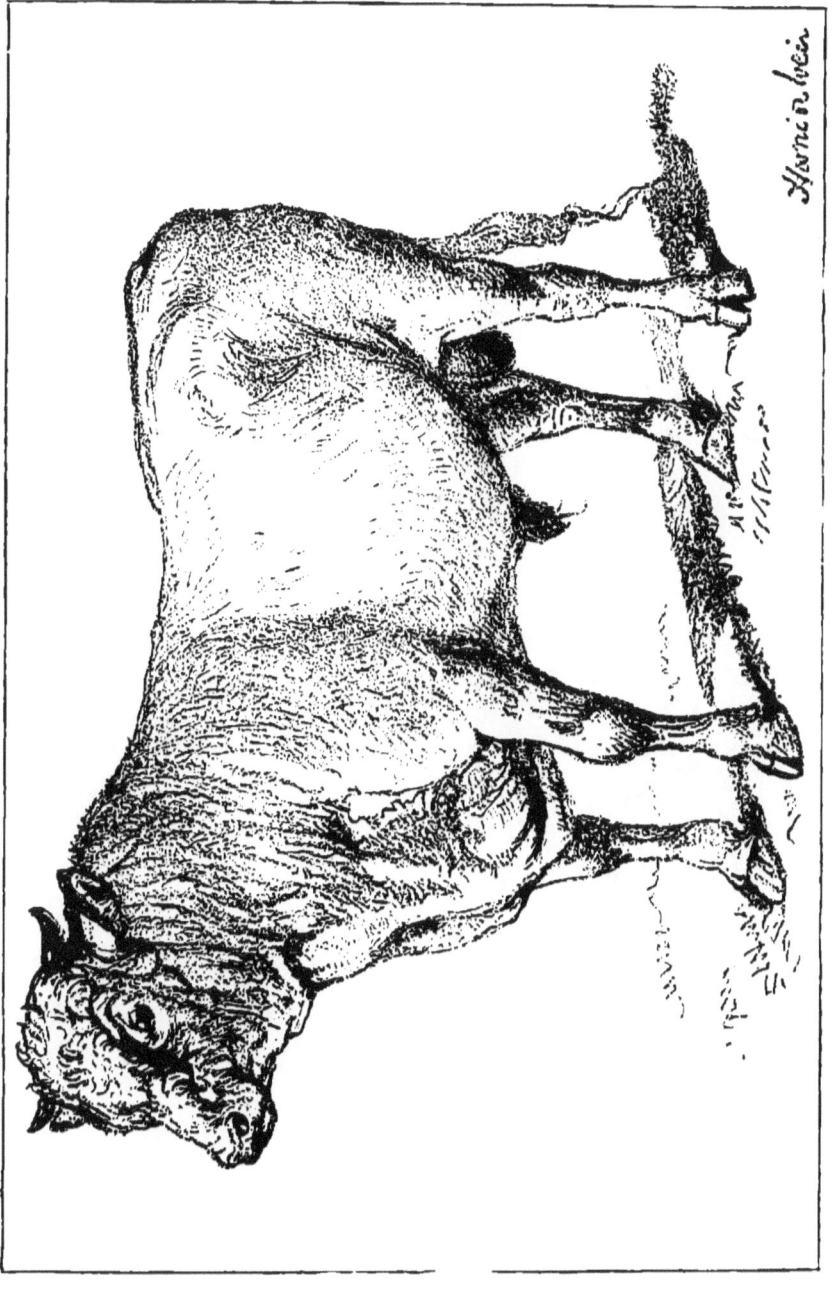

"KING CHARMING," SHORTHORN BULL.

sisted in calling her "All Butter"; while he called my Chevalier barley the "Shrivelled ear." When I was judging farming in Worcestershire the owner of one of the competing farms recommended us to eat one of his pears, which he called the Bronchitis; we discovered, on looking at the label, it was the "Bon Chrétien." But, for an excellent misnomer, the following always commended itself to me:—The Clerk of the Peace for the county of Bucks had a very good garden, and was accustomed to present the Chairman of Quarter Sessions each quarter with a bunch of a well-known rose, called *La Rose des Quatre Saisons;* his gardener always persisted in calling it the "Rose of the Quarter Sessions."

Poultry-breeding and rearing has for many years been a special hobby of mine. I have contributed occasionally papers on this subject to the Farmers' Club, and in 1885, I think it was, I stated my views and experiences in the matter to a representative of the *Daily News*, who appeared in the midst of the Chiltern Hills on interviewing bent.

It is often asked why we should pay hard money out of the country for what might be grown in it? Why, when we have plenty of corn, do we not feed more fowls? In 1884 we imported £2,908,927 worth of eggs, or nine times as much in value as in 1859, and poultry to the amount of £669,604, or about ten and a half times as much as twenty-five years ago. Why have we no great poultry farms? No doubt our production of poultry and eggs might be considerably increased, but an England *all poultry farm* is just as absurd an idea as an England all pasture, all orchard, or all market-garden.

I know of no single instance in which a large poultry farm has been successful. To begin with, poultry are very sensitive to variations of climate and the character of the soil on which they are raised. But granted that the conditions needful for a great poultry farm are all that could be desired or expected in this country, there are other difficulties. One of these, easily overlooked except by those having technical knowledge, is that, where many head of poultry are kept, of finding sufficient animal food on any given area. A fowl is not only a graminivorous, but a carnivorous or insectivorous creature, and requires a certain quantity of animal food, such as the larvæ of insects, which it pursues and hunts for with extraordinary avidity. Now, even admitting that the area of the poultry run is in the beginning wide enough to supply sufficient insect-food, the demand increases as its square year by year, but the tendency of a poultry farm is to exterminate the insects. So soon as you have to go out and buy food you are no longer likely to make a profit. As many pigs as can be fed on the refuse of a farm, with a little grain, meal, or "toppings," and a few beans occasionally bought, will return a profit, and so will the poultry, which can be maintained out of odds and ends; but I would not recommend any person to buy food by the ton to feed poultry. It would not pay, inasmuch as it would be impossible to compete against the price of Russian or of French fowls. To raise poultry largely the population also requires education, just as to grow fruit. The picking and packing of fruit and the dressing of fowls for the market do not come by instinct, like driving a gig and the rest of it ; but at the same time it is essentially the work of a small farmer, yeoman, or cottager, who can do very well by as much poultry as his wife can look after. In Ireland almost every peasant rears a clutch of geese, a brood of turkeys, or keeps at least a few fowls, and the animals do exceedingly well. This is because they roost either actually in the peasant's cabin, where there is a fire, or in a lean-to shanty into which the heat penetrates. They thus receive personal attention when young, and are not left to take care of themselves and fight against cold and wet. This is a strong example in favour, so far as poultry is concerned, of *la petite culture* against large farms; and certainly in this country also, yeomen's or cottagers' fowls seem to do better than those raised on a larger scale. It is likely enough that farmers dislike their labourers keeping any large quantity of poultry lest they are tempted to purloin corn ; fowl-growing and egg-selling are businesses in themselves, extras, as it were, on a small homestead. France, with her army of small farmers, proprietors or leaseholders, naturally raises a vastly greater quantity of poultry per square mile than can be the case in England. The majority of our barndoor fowls, it must be admitted, are mongrels, but we have some fine poultry in this country—better, I think, than in France. The French, however, not only dress their poultry better for the market, but cook it better than we do. They stuff their fowls with fresh butter before roasting them, and baste them continually. One rarely tastes a good roast fowl in England, more for want of culinary knowledge than want of good poultry.

As layers and for the table, game-fowl have hardly an equal. Their eggs and flesh are both perfect, and for beauty a black-breasted red is quite at the head of the list. But they fight so terribly that nothing else can live near them. The coming fowl is, I think, the Indian game, a bird like an improved Malay. It first turned up in Devonshire, having been brought by ship to the ports of that county. The Indian game, as it is called, is now a fixed type; they lay the finest egg, and continuously, and the chickens are so hardy as to be unkillable by the ordinary diseases and accidents to which chicks are liable. My brother brought from Madras an Indian game cock and hen from Ootacamund. They were blue in colour. We crossed them with our Indian game, and have a stock of very fine birds. I have exported many of these—several cockerels to Monte Video. Another capital race is the Plymouth Rocks, bred by the Americans from, I think, a cuckoo-coloured fowl and the Cochin. The legs are now clean, clear from feathers, but the head, tail, and roaring crow of the Cochin remain; they lay brown or buff eggs like the Cochin, but always lighter in colour. These handsome yellow-legged birds are good layers and excellent mothers, and with the Indian game make the hardiest and handiest stock for a farm. The Leghorns, too, are among the best of the varieties recently introduced. These are almost everlasting layers, producing eggs throughout the year, and lay very large fine eggs, larger than those of any other sort I know. Hamburghs, also, are good layers, but the Leghorn and Minorca eggs are the heaviest by a good deal, and are driving the Hamburghs out of the market. The laying power is all important. New-laid eggs always fetch a good price, and cannot be competed against by the foreign or "box" eggs. There is an erroneous impression that, as of common butter, comparatively stale eggs are good enough for cooking. They may serve, but they are not so good as those a day old, just as the better the butter the fitter it is for cooking, especially for basting poultry. The difference again in an omelette is very marked: when made with fresh eggs it is incomparably lighter, more fluid and digestible, than when made from those four or five days old, not to say older.

A collector of eggs at Aylesbury, who sent about 3,000 weekly to London, told me that he got better eggs from cottages than from farmers, who are not particular enough as to the variety of poultry they keep. The average, extending over the whole year, of Miss Morris's Plymouth Rocks and Dorkings, with other varieties selected for early laying, is 93 per head. Higher averages have been made by some kinds. Pure Minorcas have averaged 150, and I believe the Leghorns and Spanish varieties, if well attended to, might rival this high figure. In this country eggs are sold by the score, but in America by weight, and this American plan would be a good one to introduce into our country. A score of common farm-yard eggs will weigh about 2 lbs., but a score Leghorns 3 lbs., or half as much again. This, allowing a well-cared-for Leghorn hen to lay 140 eggs in the year, would give 21 lbs., against 14 lbs. laid by the farm-yard hen.

Various strains of poultry are suited to various

localities. Spanish have been neglected of late, but they are excellent for stable-yards and about suburbs, where they pick up a living. They were once highly fancied for their large eggs and delicate flesh, but they never sit. White Leghorns, with their beautiful scarlet combs and wattles and yellow legs, appear to great advantage when there is a grass run, but look grimy where the black Spanish thrive. The game bantam and Pekin bantams are charming creatures. Yokohamas are purely ornamental, but the little Japanese silkies are valuable for sitting on pheasants' or partridges' eggs on account of their light weight. Of the French kinds the Crèvecœurs, Houdans, and La Flèche are the birds which produce the famous capons and poulardes for the Paris market. The La Flèche variety has been tried in England, but mostly without success. They require care, I believe, and therefore thrive best among a peasant proprietary.

The Prebendal Farm was as noted for the geese I reared upon it as, I think I may say without conceit, it was celebrated for its ducks and fowls. At Birmingham in 1883 I showed a goose weighing 34 lbs., and at the Amsterdam Exhibition a gander weighing 33 lbs. and a goose 32 lbs., or of quite double the size of what would be deemed a very fine goose in any market. I introduced with success various foreign species of ducks—the Pekins with their deep orange-coloured bills and golden white plumage, hardy in nature and rapid in growth, the Cayuga, from the State of New York, the perfection of a winter duck, a prolific layer of eggs, of a large size and weight when mature, a superb black plumage, fine dark flesh, even better in flavour than that of an ordinary wild duck; but of course the pure Aylesbury strain was what I most cultivated.

All round Aylesbury the cottagers keep their "set of ducks." It is these whose snow-white plumage the tourist admires on the river Thame. They are driven home at night and well looked after. The eggs are hatched out by Dorking or Cochin China hens, for ducks are bad sitters. Often the eggs are sold to a "ducker," who gets them hatched, and then raises and fattens the young ducks, sometimes four or five thousand head in a season. These young ducklings are very carefully and artificially fed, first on hard-boiled eggs chopped fine with rice and mixed with finely-chopped bullock's liver, and afterwards with barley-meal and tallow greaves, with perhaps a little horseflesh; their life extends over only eight or nine weeks, and of the joys of pond and river they have no experience. The Aylesbury duckling has, or rather had, no competitor. In the beginning of the season he used to be worth some eighteen shillings per couple, later in the season eleven or thirteen.

The pure Aylesbury breed, long-bodied, white plumage, without spot, with pale, flesh-coloured bill and bright orange-coloured legs and feet, is prized everywhere for its great size, delicacy, and merchantable quality. A white duck always looks cleaner when plucked, and is consequently more saleable than a darker-hued one. But the pure Aylesburys seem to lose their "points" in other places; it is a purely local breed. The first sign of degeneracy is the appearance of dark spots or splashes on the bill. About Aylesbury there is abundance of what is locally called duck-gravel, a deposit like pumice-stone, into which the ducks push their bills. Every ducker's place has a lump of this duck-gravel, a coralline stuff like little oyster-shells. This is exported to other places, but the ducks do not seem to thrive so well elsewhere, and their bills soon lose their delicacy of colour.

The first year of my farming experiences, 1853, was noted as the "wet year"; it was nearly my ruin; I had a farm of 200 acres flooded seven times in six months; my hay was carried away down the river, my corn sprouted in the ear, and I lost 200 sheep by the liver rot. The glanders destroyed all my horses, my cattle scarcely put any fat on to their carcases, and in the end I found myself £1200 poorer than when I began. The following year rumours of war sprang up, and I possessed a splendid breadth of wheat, as, despite the covenants of my lease, I had sown with wheat nearly all my ploughed land. The Crimean War broke out, and my crop was sold at nearly 80s. a quarter, and recouped me nearly £600 of my former loss.

Of stringent covenants in a lease, now happily almost extinct, I must tell a good story of a London lawyer, who went down into the country as agent for a certain landlord, knowing as much of agriculture as a tenant would of Chancery practice. He went over the farm at harvest with the tenant, book in hand, to note down the various croppings in each field. On entering one of the fields they came to a heavy crop of oats, and on reference to his book, the lawyer found it had been used for *white* corn crop the year before, and the growth of two white crops in succession was forbidden by the lease. He called the tenant's attention to the fact, who, rather a wag in his way, took the Cockney on one side, and said, "Don't show your ignorance before the men; look here, sir," and then rubbing out several ears of oats in his hand, and blowing the chaff away, a fine sample of *black oats* was discovered, to the great astonishment of the lawyer, who was perfectly satisfied that the farmer had kept well within the terms of the lease, and had not grown two white corn crops in succession!

CHAPTER XVI.

A Poor Law Guardian—The Curse of Out-door Relief—The Fortunes of Agriculture—Harvest Homes—Allotments and Gardens—Steam and Spade—The Virtues of Co-operation—Since 1830—The Swing Riots—Cottage Accommodation—The Smock Frock and the Black Coat—The Archdeacon and Potatoes—The Better Part.

IN the year 1871 I consented to serve as guardian of the poor, and went to my first meeting of the board deeply imbued with the importance of my duties, and full of sympathy for the applicants. Our chairman and vice-chairman were both excellent, kindly neighbours, one a retired farmer from an adjoining village, the other a grazier, a man of property, resident in the town. Under their guidance and management the rates of the Union were extremely heavy, the mass of the labouring people paupers, and the out-door relief had risen to a very high average, as compared with some of the best-managed Unions. Not many weeks after my election, I began to have my misgivings as to the humanitarianism of this system, and, in conjunction with several of my brother guardians, we were determined that a complete alter-ation should be attempted, and, in direct opposition to our chairman, we insisted on a more vigorous application of the workhouse test. We were soon rewarded by a

THE POOR LAW.

diminution of rates, as well as a reduction in the number of applicants for relief, so that by the end of the year the Union rate was reduced 20 per cent., and the number of paupers receiving out-door relief was diminished in proportion. We made another alteration by the compulsion exercised on the children of paupers to contribute to the maintenance of their parents. It really surprised me to find Englishmen, perhaps paupers for years, receiving 3*s.* to 5*s.* per week from the rates whose sons were in business, some of them better off than many guardians on the board. These scamps, as soon as they were threatened with a summons, at once took their parents off the pay list. Others, again—young, hearty agricultural labourers, single men, earning from 14*s.* to 16*s.* per week, when such wages went further than larger sums nowadays—refused to contribute a farthing to the support of an aged father or mother, not even having the excuse of belonging to some club, in most instances lodging themselves with brothers or sisters, and paying perhaps not more than 1*s.* per week for their lodging, spending the remainder of their earnings entirely upon themselves. I have now been a guardian many years, and have seen the poor rate—the rate raised especially for the poor—reduced more than one-half; the poor themselves are better off, and a healthier feeling is springing up amongst the agricultural labourers in the district; the proper spirit of pride slowly asserting itself, has developed amongst them a desire to be above dependence upon the parish. Much of this feeling has no doubt been caused by the higher wages of the field labourer, much by the improved system of education,

—which, retarded as it has been by the obstinate indifference of those who should have been better advised, has still made steady progress—but still more by the better administration of the law, especially in reference to the restrictions of out-door relief. I believe the Poor Law of England to have been framed on benevolent principles, but I have no doubt it has engendered amongst the wage-earning class that utter thriftlessness which led to the downfall and almost to the destruction of the principle of independence; it absolutely broke up all feelings of filial affection, it has fostered imprudent marriages, and has destroyed many of the most honourable feelings of domestic life.

The more I examine into the position of the agricultural labourer, the more I am convinced of the utter demoralization caused by the Poor Law; from its commencement to the present time, the same baneful results are to be found pervading nearly every relation of country life. In the beginning of the history of the last fifty years of my life miserably low wages were supplemented by the rates, the agricultural labourer was a mere serf tied to his parish, entirely in the hands of the farmer, who in his turn was generally, from his isolation in country districts, a self-opinionated, obstinate man, objecting to all interference with his jog-trot routine, believing that the groove in which he moved was the be-all and end-all of his existence, and if any advice was offered him, he surely spurned it with contempt. The farmers' position and opinions were winked at by the resident landlord, who seemed to be content to be the lord of the land, without the responsibilities of the landlord, whilst the parish clergyman, wishing to be on good terms with all classes, readily acquiesced in the usual parochial system ; and yet, in spite of this species of mental stagnation, rural England was happy in her institutions, and gloried in her country life. All parties seemed to be bound together in their parish existence, and when the rivalry of adjoining parishes was stimulated by the annual cricket-match or the bell-ringing of treble bob majors, everything connected with the event was carried out with mutual good-humour. The squire and the parson, with their families, especially the lady department, spread refinement amongst the homes of their tenants, and a portion of that refinement entered the dwellings of the poor. But the advent of that mighty reformer, the steam-engine, coursing along through many a secluded hamlet, and the inevitable railway station, created a restlessness and almost a rebellion against established customs, and brought what is called civilization and enlightenment amongst the primitive inhabitants. Artificial manure, "gohanner," as the immortal Jorrocks called it, took the place of the old farm-yard muck ; oil-cake, locust-beans and various spiced feeding stuffs, all of them tending to enrich the land, were brought almost to the doors of many of the more intelligent farmers. The schoolmaster was abroad ; books were published, local newspapers started, advocating opinions which forced new ideas into the houses of all farmers as well as of the landlords. This great outburst of kindling fire illumined the darkest recesses of every country village as much as it did the manufacturing town ; the countrymen were slower perhaps to appreciate the benefits of science, but, when once aroused, their spirit of enterprise bore a favourable comparison with the much-lauded manufacturing brother. The best instance of this is in the support given to the manufacture of agricultural implements, which in its importance not only to England, but to her colonies, and to the whole world, rivals that of the most celebrated inventions for the manufacture of cotton, wool, or hardware. The introduction of the steam cultivator by a Buckinghamshire tenant-farmer, W. Smith of Wolstone, commenced a new era in the history of agriculture, an invention further improved upon by Fowler of Leeds and Howard of Bedford, followed by the steam thrasher, and this again followed, in its turn, by improved reaping and mowing machines,—all proving unmistakeably that the fire of enterprise was not dead, and only needed the spark to kindle it into a flame.

The establishment in 1839 of the Royal Agricultural Society of England was the outcome of many important local agricultural associations, around which, as a centre, landlords, tenants, men of science, manufacturers, and the general public could circulate their opinions, and put in practice many of their theories, and it raised the tone of agriculture most materially. Agriculture thrived, land soon went up in value, the landlord had more money to spend in trade, the farmer's home was improved, his children were better educated, the labourer's wages were increased, his dwelling was made more habitable—when suddenly these halcyon days were rudely ended by the intrusion of the Irish famine. The miseries endured by a whole people brought home to the mind

FORTUNES OF AGRICULTURE.

of the statesman who then ruled the destiny of England, Sir R. Peel, that it was wrong to tax the food of the masses, and the repeal of the Corn Laws was the outcome of this conviction. At first "a heavy blow, and great discouragement" fell on the cultivators of the land, the years 1848—1852 were very disastrous, many cultivators were ruined, and the price of wheat fell from the average of 69s. 5d. in 1847 to 38s. 7d. in 1851.

The years 1852 and 1853 witnessed the same calamity that oppressed us again in 1879 and 1880 in their continuous rains and floods, rotting the sheep and destroying the crops. Then came the good harvests of 1854, 1855, and 1856; the Russian War stopped the supplies of corn from the Black Sea and the Baltic, and the price of wheat rose respectively to 72s. 7d., 74s. 9d., 89s. 2d. I myself sold in 1856 a considerable quantity of fine wheat at 100s. per quarter; little attention was at that time bestowed upon American produce, but we have lived to see how the application of steam machinery both on land and sea has annihilated space; the European supply of agricultural products has fallen off, but the importation of American corn and meat has grown to gigantic proportions; with bad harvests, the partial destruction of our herds by pleuro-pneumonia and foot-and-mouth disease following that direful scourge the rinderpest, and during some of the past years the frightful loss of our flocks by liver rot—with all this added to lowering of prices, I fear many of our best farmers have been ruined, and under present circumstances there seems little or no hope of amelioration. But I trust that, as before, when times are at the worst they begin to mend, and that the pluck and determination of the British farmer will, under a merciful Providence, carry him through the present deplorable state of his affairs. He is being met in a liberal spirit by his landlord, who year after year does not hesitate to lower his rents, aids him in the improvement of his buildings, consents to his having entire freedom of cultivation, grants more liberal covenants, and sanctions a more reasonable agreement on the basis of the Agricultural Holdings Act. At the same time I hold that the burthens, which now so heavily and most unfairly press on the land, must be removed, the highway rates must be more fairly apportioned, the charge for the maintenance of the poor and the insane be placed on a wider basis, and we may yet see agriculture itself again, and Old England will once more become

"Great, glorious, and free,
First flower of the earth, and first gem of the sea."

One feature of old country life is fast vanishing from our sight, I mean the old-fashioned harvest-home festival, which long was kept up at most of the farm-houses in the country, especially among the well-to-do tenantry. I mention my own, not perhaps as a sample, because living in a town and having other business operations, it was scarcely a typical gathering; but my father, for some years previously to his death living at his quiet homestead, which was situated about two miles from the town, was about as fair a specimen of a tenant-farmer as could be found in the county. His custom was to invite some of the village tradesmen, such as the blacksmith, wheelwright, and carpenter, to join the festive throng, and these, with about twenty of the labourers, old and young, formed with the family a company of about forty persons; my father took the head of the table, myself the bottom end. A round of beef and a haunch of mutton, with a goodly addition of plum-pudding, formed the cheer, with plenty of good beer, and, after grace had been said, pipes and tobacco were placed on the table, and an address referring to the harvest and the prospects of the coming year used to be delivered with great propriety by my worthy father, who was an excellent speaker. The song and joke went round, and after about half an hour had been spent in such convivial interchanges, the men now being well warmed to their work, the following ceremony took place: Three of the men sitting near each other stood up, whilst one of the others, selected as a tolerably good singer, struck up the following stanza—

"Here's a health unto our master, the founder of the feast,
I hope to God with all my heart his soul in heaven may rest,
And all his works may prosper that e'er he takes in hand,
For we are all his servants, and all at his command—
So drink, boys, drink, and see you do not spill,
For if you do you shall drink two, for 'tis our master's will."

Each of the three men standing up held a cup containing half a pint of beer in his hand, and at the words "Drink, boys, drink," they had to gulp down the nut-brown beverage, the bystanders watching intently to see if any drop was spilled, for then the double penalty was surely inflicted. This performance always occasioned great fun, and then toast, speech, and song went on till near midnight, when most of the guests took their departure for their homes in the village, which was about a mile distant, but several of them lay down in the barn or stable that they might be ready for their work the next morning.

I regret to have to admit that the chief number of the company before their departure were generally intoxicated, although merry and full of fun; it would have been against the spirit and public opinion of the time to have sent one's guests home sober. One man told me, as a criterion of good beer, "he didn't think nothing of no beer if it did not give him three falls for a shilling." When travelling on the Continent I had been struck with the absence of drunkenness amongst the country folk, so I thought I would try the use of claret and water, made into a nicely-flavoured claret cup, at the next convivial gathering of labouring folk at home. Instead of offering so much beer, I made three or four gallons of liquor by putting two quarts of water to one quart of good sound wine costing about 1s. 2d., and with a slice or two of lemon, a little nutmeg and a quarter of a pound of sugar, I made a beverage which cost rather under 6d. per quart. In proposing her Majesty's health after supper, I told them what I had seen in France, especially after the vintage, and that they should be free to try and use wine instead of beer. I placed tumblers and jugs of "cup" on the table along with the mugs and tankard of beer, and I found that more than half the men preferred the claret cup and stuck to it during the evening, and told me next day how well they felt and how much they preferred it to beer, but I do not pretend that in the hay or harvest-field it would have been so popular, besides which, there is the expense to be considered.

I generally managed to have my harvest home the day after the Town Horticultural Show and banquet, for which London professional singers were engaged, and I usually succeeded in persuading some of them to stay and enjoy "a day in the country," and improve, besides, the harmony of our evening; they would enjoy the quaint rustic songs of the labourers, and themselves would sing such fine old glees as "The Chough and Crow," "Life's a Bumper," "Glorious Apollo." In my employment was a deaf man, much appreciated as a singer; on one of these occasions, one of my men having sung a dreary composition of inordinate length, which thoroughly bored his audience, his deaf neighbour was called upon to follow him, when, to the horror and dismay of every one, he struck up the very same ditty which had so tired the company just before; shouting and demonstration alike failed to make the deaf man understand the predicament, and he droned out the whole of the dreary song to the bitter end.

I persuaded Douglas Jerrold to attend one of these annual festivals, to whom a joke had introduced me. I had been in the habit of jotting down in a diary any racy or interesting scraps which I had chanced upon in a newspaper, and Douglas Jerrold was looking through this book, and seemed much amused at one extract in particular; handing it to his friend, at whose house he was staying, and with whom he had come to my father's, then laughing heartily, he told me that he was the author of it: "Women, when maids, are m'ld as milk; once make them wives, and they lean their backs against their marriage certificate and defy you." But my harvest celebrations did not only consist of song and joke; I tried to make the pleasant gatherings of more permanent use, by shortly commenting on the position of agriculture and explaining to my men any new inventions or improvements which had been adopted during the year.

On taking my farm I determined to do my utmost to improve the position of my labourers. I apportioned a certain section of the farm to be used as allotments for the labourers working thereon. I am now speaking of the year 1853, and I kept up the system up to the time I gave up the farm in 1879; for those twenty-six years I found it had a marvellously good and beneficial effect. I gave the men the very best land on the farm, and close to the homestead and farmyard; they were charged the same amount per acre that I paid myself, with the rates and taxes added; no man had less than a rood, nor more than half an acre, as I found practically that this was quite as much as a man and his family could cultivate, and that it amply supplied the family with vegetables for their own consumption, and oftentimes left them with an abundance over to sell. They had full permission to fetch whatever amount of manure they required from my farmyard, I, on my part, making it a condition that their holdings should be well-cultivated and kept clean. On my harvest-home festival we had a horticultural show of all the garden produce; I put the rents of their holdings together, which were supplemented by the gift of a sovereign from my landlord and of the same sum by my wife, who ever took the greatest personal interest in the well-being of the wives and children of the men, and I then distributed the amount in prizes for their produce. The specimens of their vegetables were splendid, and my labourers were generally most successful at the Horticultural Society's Show in the town. With little expense nearly every farmer throughout England, if he will only take the trouble, might benefit in the same way the men he employs on the land, and endear them to the soil they are helping to cultivate by giving them an interest in part of it; the only essential is that, where this plan is carried out, the gardens should be as near as possible to the homestead, as the men after a hard day's work, naturally, do not like to walk a mile there and back to their allotment ground, and they should, besides, have every opportunity of getting manure easily. I set apart four acres out of 200 for this purpose, and I never regretted it, and felt sure it benefited me as much as the men, as they were always fresh to their work, and were certain to be on the spot whenever they were wanted.

In co-operation I found another feature in which the lot of the agricultural labourer could be largely ameliorated, and be made of immense service to his employer at but little expense. My purpose was to encourage the men to do their best with the machinery I purchased and employed on the farm. When I first became convinced that steam culture was *un fait accompli*, I went to Mr. Howard's, of Bedford, and bought my own set of steam-tackle, the system of Smith, of Wolstone; my engine I hired from the man who threshed my corn, giving him £1 a day for the hire; my ploughman rode on the cultivator, and to him I gave, in addition to his full weekly wage, 3d. an acre on all he cultivated, and, as he did about five acres a day, he earned an extra six shillings a week; the anchor men, and all others employed at that work, also had so much an acre, the result being that they worked as long in the evenings as it was possible to see, and started as early as they could be about in the morning; if the work was scamped, it was my fault. When the mowing-machine was brought out, I was the first in the county of Bucks to purchase and use one; it was an American machine, one of Walter Wood's, a really good machine, although it would be laughed at now, so great, since that time, have been the improvements in agricultural implements. When I determined on purchasing this machine I sent for my carter, who had hitherto been the head of a gang of five mowers, and who not only mowed mine, but also the crops of my neighbours, and found on inquiry that they could, by extremely hard labour, earn about 30s. a week in haytime, they finding their own beer. I then broke the ice, and told him I was going to give him a carriage and pair of horses to drive, and that for the future he would earn as much as a coachman as he was earning then by dragging himself to pieces by mowing; he could not understand what I meant, but I told him to prepare a new set of leather reins, and to have ready a pair of his most active horses. Then, one day, Mr. Cranston, of the firm of Walter Wood and Co., arrived with the mower, the horses were harnessed to it,

CO-OPERATION IN FARMING. 257

and, Mr. Cranston driving, they dashed through the gateway into the standing grass, levelling it as they went, to the unbounded surprise of Jem, my carter, and of all my numerous friends who had assembled to witness the result. Jem now in turn took his seat, and after a few lessons he drove it remarkably well, mowing upwards of a hundred acres that year, including clover and meadow grass, without an accident. I gave him 6d. an acre and four pints of beer a day; in this way he earned considerably more than he could have done by mowing with his scythe, so he was content to become a gentleman, driving his carriage and pair, throughout haytime. When the reaping-machine came out in a good form, I repeated the same tactics; to all the men I gave extra pay, and they regarded with good will every labour-saving machine I afterwards purchased and used.

The most successful application of co-operation was, I found, in regard to the production of live stock on the farm and their exhibition at Agricultural Shows. My cowman had 5s. a head for all the calves he reared on the farm; the shepherd had 6d. for every lamb, about 160 being reared annually; the carter 10s. for every colt reared, and 20 per cent. on all prizes won by the stock at the shows. Each man had an interest in the earnings of the farm and in its produce and crops. When I won a prize for the cultivation of root crops, and for the best samples of wheat, barley, or beans, or for the general cultivation on the farm, I divided 20 per cent. of the sum so obtained between all the men on the farm. I think most strongly that this method of dealing with

s

workmen might be carried out to a much greater extent in agriculture than it is at present, with very beneficial results; but then I am, it is true, speaking of the halcyon days of farming, and not of the depressed industry, as it now exists, in all parts of the country.

In the period from the year 1830 onwards will be found most of the great alterations that have taken place in the science and practice and position of agriculture; the discoveries of chemical science as to manures, the invention of the steam cultivator, the introduction of the mowing and reaping-machine, the rise of the vast establishments for the manufacturing of every variety of agricultural machinery, the abolition of the Corn Laws, the fearful outbreaks of the cattle plague or rinderpest, the great improvement in the breeds of cattle, especially of shorthorns, the influence of railways on agriculture—all these circumstances have had an important bearing on country life. Yet, notwithstanding the lamentable depression of agriculture just now, men who can remember the years of 1831-32, and look back on the troubles which the farmers surmounted then, may hope the time is not far distant when success will again crown their efforts.

When I was at school in 1831, every farm in the parish of Aylesbury was untenanted and in the hands of the landlord, whilst the pitiably bad management of the Poor Law had pauperized nearly the whole working population of the kingdom. In this year I was accustomed to look from my bed-room window at Uxbridge School and see, on many a night, three or four blazing homesteads. These troublous times culminated in the rising of the

THE SWING RIOTS.

agricultural labourers. Bodies of lawless men marched from village to village, breaking up every machine invented for the saving of labour. The farmers and trading classes were powerless to control them; the yeomanry were called out, and special constables were sworn in to suppress the "Swing riots," as they were styled, from the threatening letters which farmers received warning them that their farms would be destroyed, and signed "Swing," in allusion, probably, to the penalty of hanging for arson. Along the valley of the Colne, and especially in the Wycombe valley, many of the paper-mills were gutted, the machinery smashed, and the town of Wycombe and district got into the hands of a lawless mob. At that time a pack of staghounds was kept in the neighbourhood of Uxbridge, and was hunted by a right good master, Mr. Sullivan. One day, the deer having been taken at West Wycombe, the well-mounted field of horsemen were returning through the town, and found the place practically in the hands of a ruffianly mob, which the local authorities were powerless to combat. The high-spirited master of the hounds called on his companions to follow him, and with the butt-ends of their hunting-whips they slashed in amongst the mob, drove them helter-skelter out of the town, took several prisoners, and delivered the borough from their depredations.

These unfortunate outbreaks lasted for several weeks, and then, in nearly every part of the county, a special Commission of Assize was held, and at Aylesbury scores of misguided men were arraigned for riot and arson, were mostly found guilty and sentenced to various terms of imprisonment and transportation, and the country became gradually quieted. Among others, two men, whose names I forbear to mention, were tried for these crimes and sentenced to death, but three days before the time fixed for execution they received a reprieve, and the sentence was commuted to transportation for life. One died in New South Wales, and the other, a tall, fine agricultural labourer, received a pardon after having served several years of his sentence. He returned to his native parish, and became a thriving man; and a few years ago, whilst I was in the Assize Court, I saw this very man a prosecutor giving evidence against a prisoner who had robbed him, and who was of course standing in the dock, in the very same place where the prosecutor had stood some years before and had heard himself sentenced to death!

I have omitted to state one serious cause of the maladministration of the old Poor Law, due, I regret to say, to scandalous behaviour of many landowners during the early part of the present century—this was the system of pulling down and destroying the cottages on an estate, and by this means driving the labourers into other parishes, so as to get rid of the cost of the maintenance of the poor altogether, especially in old age. I have even known instances in which the parish church was for a like reason permitted to fall into decay. Quarrendon, near Aylesbury, is an instance; and the clergyman, who was non-resident, and whose duty it was to serve the parish, took no action, as it saved him the trouble of going from his residence to a parish two miles off; thus also the farmers got rid of the church-rates; and,

COTTAGE ACCOMMODATION.

in the instance I have alluded to, they used the beams of the church to make gate-posts, and broke down the walls to repair their gateways. I once made a calculation of the number of miles that a very deserving and clever herdsman of one of our leading graziers in this parish had walked in going to and from his work during the time he had lived with him, being nearly fifty years. I proved he had walked three times round the world to do his duty to his master! I told the man's master of this fact, and he replied, "I can't help it, there are but three cottages in the parish"—a parish of over 2000 acres. I remember that I wrote to *The Times* detailing these circumstances as an instance of the short-sighted policy of both landlords and tenants in permitting such a state of things.

The smock-frock farmer has almost ceased to exist, but some still survive and hold small occupations of from fifty to a hundred acres, leading an industrious, hard-faring life, living ofttimes more frugally than their labourers, and going on, as the saying is on the Chiltern Hills, "from cherry-time to cherry-time," and getting "no forrarder." Fresh meat to them is a Sunday and market-day luxury; but to say that a man cannot rise from the labouring ranks is to state what is contrary to the fact. I have known myself instances of successful countrymen. One man I recollect had started life as a plough-boy, was a saving lad, began dealing in pigs, then kept a horse and cart, and followed what was called "higgling," buying eggs and poultry, and with a little carrying of goods to various market towns, and an occasional journey to London, saved money enough to take a small farm, and by degrees, with great industry and perseverance, added to his farm till he became the tenant of 300 acres, and the owner himself of 100 more acres, besides of several cottages. He brought up a large family of sons, and placed them into farms, dying, a few years since, a well-to-do man. He could neither read nor write; and one New Year's Day he brought me his banker's pass-book—at the time money had been very dear, up to 10 or 12 per cent.—and told me how handsomely his bankers had behaved to him, as they had that day made him a present of three five-pound notes for having kept a good balance in their hands. I looked at his pass-book, and found the average balance through the year had been nearly £1200! No wonder his banker could afford to give him £15. He was churchwarden of his parish, and had a serious quarrel with the parish clerk, a drunken fellow, and I advised him to write to the Archdeacon of Buckingham and get the clerk dismissed. "*That'll never do*," said Johnny, "for he's the only man in parish as can read the sarvice."

Archdeacon of Buckingham! He lived at Shanklin in the Isle of Wight, and was only to be seen in Buckinghamshire once in two or three years. At one of these parochial visitations, few and far between, he went into a certain church and was shown round by the sexton, the rector being from home at the time. On entering the churchyard he found about half of it dug up and planted with potatoes, and the Archdeacon, much horrified, exclaimed, "What, what! Potatoes, potatoes! This is very wrong, very wrong indeed!" "Yes, sir," says the sexton, "I tould measter 'twere wrong, for it were taters last year, and taters the year afore, and it ought to have bin wheat this year."

Another archidiaconal story, from Suffolk. The Archdeacon, when visiting a certain parish, asked the parish clerk what sort of man the rector was; the clerk, looking hard at the lectern with the eagle and out-stretched wings, and at the same time pointing to the pulpit, replied, " Well, sir, he ain't much in the tub, but he's stunning behind the goose," or "geuse" as the Suffolk vernacular has it. Country folk are seldom lacking in the quality of a certain dry humour. In the neighbourhood of Tring, on the Chiltern Hills, lived one of those small farmers who had been apparently very successful in life, and had the reputation of being a moneyed man, but who had gained his cash in a very doubtful manner, and his neighbours did not hesitate to discuss that manner. One day this farmer was enjoying his pipe over a pint of ale in a village public. To him a rather plain, eccentric character, rejoicing in the sobriquet of Bunker—" I say, Master David, I took your part t'other day; I stood up for you, I did." " Did you, Bunker?" said David. " That was very kind of you. How did you take my part?" To him again, Bunker— " Well, I was having a pipe with a man near St. Albans, who said he knowed a man who had seed a man as had stole more sheep than you had ; and I said he was a liar." It may be well imagined that David went home a sadder, if not a wiser man, determined not again to invite the confidences of Bunker.

After the year 1835 a marked improvement rapidly took place, both in the habits of the tenants, in the management of their farms, in their households, and in the general style of their living. The farmers, their wives and families, began to dress as well as their fellows in the towns, and in their household began to practise the social amenities of life; the farmer rode a good horse to hounds, and the education of his family now left little to be desired. All this is as it should be. Drudgery is not the end-all of life. As a boy I saw the serviceable smock-frock give way to broadcloth, and a decent horse and trap take the place of the old market conveyances; I saw agriculture awake from days of torpor and depression and exalted into its rightful standing, as one of the great scientific industries of our nation; I have lived to see it again depressed and reduced, and once more the rural districts pervaded with a spirit of doubt and unrest and uncertainty in what the future may have in store. I make no pretence to play the part of a prophet; I merely have tried to sketch in some sort of rough outline things I myself have seen and know; but, alike to those that are disheartened and those that bestir themselves overmuch, I would quote a verse the country-folk in my day used to sing occasionally at their gatherings—

"'The race is not always got
 By them wot strive and for it run,
Nor the Battel to them peopel
 Wot's got the longest gun."

THE END.

www.ingramcontent.com/pod-product-compliance
Lightning Source LLC
Chambersburg PA
CBHW032122230426
43672CB00009B/1823